2B
SPLIT EDITION

LIVE BEAT
STUDENTS' BOOK

Ingrid Freebairn • Jonathan Bygrave • Judy Copage • Olivia Johnston • Sarah Curtis • Rod Fricker

Pearson Education Limited,
Edinburgh Gate, Harlow
Essex, CM20 2JE, England
and Associated Companies throughout the world

www.pearsonelt.com

© Pearson Education Limited 2015

The right of Jonathan Bygrave, Judy Copage, Ingrid Freebairn, Olivia Johnston and Sarah Curtis to be identified as authors of this work has been asserted by them in accordance with the Copyright, Designs and Patents Act, 1988.

First published 2015

ISBN 978-1-292-10195-8

Set in Helvetica Neue LTD Std 55 Roman 10/14 pt

Photo Acknowledgements

The publisher would like to thank the following for their kind permission to reproduce their photographs:

(Key: b-bottom; c-centre; l-left; r-right; t-top)

akg-images Ltd: The Voyage of the Mayflower-Steel engraving after the painting, c.1850, by John Marshall the Elder, colour added later. 10 (background), 10cr; **Alamy Images:** Helen Dixon 30tc, 31, photonic 17 39bc, Olaf Speier 40, Janine Wiedel Photolibrary 52r; **Bridgeman Art Library Ltd:** Pilgrim Fathers and Squanto, the friendly Indian, after an illustration by C. W. Jefferys, 1926 (colour litho), American School, (20th century) / Private Collection / Peter Newark Pictures / The Bridgeman Art Library 10br; **Corbis:** Sherrie Nickol / Citizen Stock 52l, Terra 30bc, Tetra Images 38b; **DK Images:** Claire Cordier 17/6, Nigel Hicks 17/1; **Fotolia.com:** Marco Becker 17/3, Natalia Bratslavsky 17/4, Philip Date 8b, Maksym

Dykha 39tc, Jaroslaw Grudzinski 32, ibphoto 39bl, lassedesignen 39tl, Petr Malyshev 39tr, Monkey Business 21, Ulrich Müller 17/2, PRILL Mediendesign 39cl, punsayaporn 39c, ryflip 35, RZ 20-21 (background), m. schuckart 39cr, Stas 17/5; **Getty Images:** Peter Arnold 51bl, Comstock 20l, Digital Vision 48, FOX via Getty Images 28b, Tony Woolliscroft / Wireimage 28t; **Courtesy Minack Theatre:** 30tr; **Pearson Education Ltd:** Gareth Boden 4l, 4r, 6b, 16bl, 18, 26, 38t, 45, 46t, 46bl, 46bc, 46br; **Rex Features:** 51tr, Alisdair Macdonald 6t, Varley / SIPA 50bl; **Shutterstock.com:** Dan Breckwoldt 14t, Kevin Eaves 14b, Karen Grigoryan 11, Oleksiy Mark 17/7, SBakhadirov 24cr, Shadowmac 30bl, Kiselev Andrey Valerevich 29; **SuperStock:** imagebroker.net 24b; **The Kobal Collection:** Danjaq / Eon Productions 8cr, New Line / Saul Zaentz / Wing Nut / The Kobal Collection / Vinet, Pierre 8cl, Twentieth Century-Fox Film Corporation 8tl, Universal / Playtone 8tr

Cover image: *Front*: **Shutterstock.com:** Ollyy

All other images © Pearson Education

Every effort has been made to trace the copyright holders and we apologise in advance for any unintentional omissions. We would be pleased to insert the appropriate acknowledgement in any subsequent edition of this publication.

Special thanks to the following for their help during location photography:

Riverside Ice and Leisure Centre, Chelmsford; Zagara Restaurant, Hoddesdon;

Tania Johnson; Anne Meaden; Mik Gates

Illustration Acknowledgements

(Key: b-bottom; c-centre; l-left; r-right; t-top)

David Banks; Adrian Barclay (Beehive Illustration); Kathy Baxendale; Pete Ellis; Kevin Hopgood (Beehive Illustration); Richard Jones (Beehive Illustration); Joanna Kerr; Mike Lacey (Beehive Illustration); Bob Lea; Wes Lowe (Beehive Illustration); Martin Sanders (Beehive Illustration); David Shenton; Eric Smith (KJA Artists); Tony Wilkins

Contents

Grammar Past continuous
Vocabulary Adverbs

5 DRAMA

Dialogue

1 🎧 **Listen and read. Complete the dialogue with the correct phrases.**

Kiran:	I saw Tom yesterday. He had long hair and he **was wearing** weird clothes.
Jodie:	¹___
Kiran:	²___ He **was standing** opposite his school and he **was talking** to a man in the street.
Jodie:	Are you sure it was Tom?
Kiran:	Yes, definitely. I was on the bus and I saw him clearly. The bus **wasn't going** very fast and I took a photo of him. ³___
Jodie:	Yes, that's Tom.
Kiran:	What **was** he **doing** in strange clothes on a Thursday afternoon outside his school?
Jodie:	I think I know! Their school show is tomorrow and he's playing a 1970s rock star. ⁴___ he **was trying** to sell tickets. Were people buying tickets?
Kiran:	No, they **weren't**.
Jodie:	I'm not surprised!

Phrases
• Have a look. • Honestly! • I expect
• You're winding me up!

Comprehension

2 **Answer the questions.**

1 Where was Tom?
   He was opposite his school.
2 Who was Tom talking to?
3 Where was Kiran?
4 What did Kiran do?
5 What are the tickets for?

SOLVE IT!

3 **What day is the show?**

Grammar

Past continuous	
Affirmative	**Negative**
He **was wearing** weird clothes. They **were standing** in the street.	The bus **wasn't going** fast. They **weren't wearing** weird clothes.
Yes/No questions	Short answers
Was he **wearing** a hat? **Were** they **wearing** weird clothes?	Yes, he **was**. No, he **wasn't**. Yes, they **were**. No, they **weren't**.

⟫ **Now make sentences with *I* and *we*.**

4 Read the dialogue again. Notice the words in red.

Practice

5 Look at the pictures. Why didn't they answer the phone yesterday evening? Ask and answer questions.

1 Lisa/watch/TV

   A: Was Lisa watching TV?
   B: No, she wasn't. She was listening to music.

2 Dad/cook/dinner?
3 Mum/work/on the computer?
4 Peter/do/his homework?
5 Grandma/play/the drums?

Pronunciation: /ɒ/ rock /ɔː/ saw

6 🎧 5/02 Go to page 60.

Vocabulary: Adverbs

7 🎧 5/03 Listen and repeat.

		Adjective	Adverb	Adjective	Adverb
Regular adverbs		• angry • bad • careful • careless • clear • easy	• angrily • badly • carefully • carelessly • clearly • easily	• loud • noisy • polite • quick • quiet • slow	• loudly • noisily • politely • quickly • quietly • slowly
Irregular adverbs		• early • fast • good	• early • fast • well	• hard • late	• hard • late

8 Use the adverbs to complete the dialogue.

Sam: Hi, Nick. What's the matter?

Nick: Oh, my family are so annoying. My dad sings [1]*badly* (bad) in the shower. Every morning!

Sam: Well, my brother always plays his music [2]___ (loud) when I'm trying to do my homework.

Nick: My sister's weird. She plays her music really [3]___ (quiet), but she eats really [4]___ (noisy). It's horrible.

Sam: You're lucky. We always finish our dinner [5]___ (late) because my mum eats [6]___ (slow). Every day I miss the beginning of my favourite TV show. What about your mum?

Nick: Well, she works [7]___ (hard) and cooks [8]___ (good), but she likes dancing in front of the TV! It's really embarrassing!

Listen

9 🎧 5/04 Listen to Harry talking about last night. Match a verb and an adverb to a person. Use one word from each box.

1 Harry's cousin 2 Adam 3 Mel 4 Harry 5 Poppy	worked left played the guitar sang played the drums	slowly. loudly. quietly. badly. early.

Extra practice

For more practice, go to page 54.

5b I was cycling when ...

Grammar   Past continuous and past simple
with *while* and *when*

Vocabulary   Prepositions of place and motion

Dialogue

1 🎧 **5 05** **Listen and read. What play are Kiran and Jodie going to see?**

Kiran: Why have you got blue plasters on your knees? What happened?

Jodie: I fell off my bike yesterday *while* I *was coming* home from Tom's house.

Kiran: Ouch! How did it happen?

Jodie: I *was cycling* down the hill *when* a cat *ran* across the road. I tried to stop, but the road was wet and I fell off.

Kiran: What happened to the cat?

Jodie: The cat was fine. It just ran up a tree. But I cut my knees quite badly and my bike was a mess.

Kiran: How did you get home?

Jodie: Well, fortunately, *while* I *was picking up* my bike, Dad *drove* past.

Kiran: That was lucky.

Jodie: Really lucky. He put my bike into the car and took me home.

Kiran: So are you ready for three hours of *Romeo and Juliet*? The play starts at two o'clock.

Jodie: I'm fine, but it hurts when I bend my knees.

Kiran: That's OK. We've got standing tickets. You can keep your knees straight.

Comprehension

2 **Answer true (T), false (F) or doesn't say (DS).**

1 Jodie fell off her bike. *T*
2 The cat ran up a wall.
3 It was raining.
4 Jodie went home by car.
5 They have chairs to sit on in the theatre.

SOLVE IT!

3 **What time does the play finish?**

Grammar

Past continuous and past simple with *while* and *when*
I was cycling down the hill **when** a cat **ran** across the road.   **While** I **was picking up** my bike, Dad **drove** past.

4 Read the dialogue again. Notice the words in red.

Practice

5 Complete the text with the past continuous or past simple form of a word from the box.

> • see • shop • eat • text • run • order
> • pick up • drop

Clare ¹*was shopping* yesterday in town when she
²___ her friend Zoe. They were hungry so they
went to a café. While Clare ³___ her boyfriend,
Zoe ⁴___ burgers and chips. The girls ⁵___ their
burgers when Clare ⁶___ her purse on the floor.
While she ⁷___ the purse, a mouse ⁸___ under the
table. Clare screamed, but Zoe just laughed.

Vocabulary: Prepositions of place and motion

6a **Recall** Name the prepositions of place in the diagrams. Then check the Word bank on page 59.

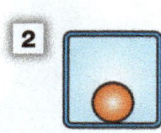

under

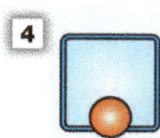

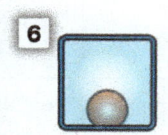

b 🎧 **Extension** Listen and repeat.

> • across • along • down • into • out of
> • over • past • through • up

7 Jenny forgot her mum's birthday. She went to the shop to buy her a present. Look at her route. Write sentences using the prompts and prepositions of place and motion.

1 climb/window
2 go/kitchen window
3 ran/garden
4 climb/wall
5 walk/street
6 go/shop

1 Jenny climbed out of the window.

Write

8 Write a short story about one of the ideas below. Use the past continuous, past simple and prepositions of place and motion.

• A funny day at school
• A terrible sports day
• An unusual Saturday

Last Saturday I was doing my homework when I saw a strange man outside my house. He was climbing over …

Extra practice

For more practice, go to page 54.

5c A dog which bends.

Grammar Defining relative clauses with *who, which* and *where*
Vocabulary Types of film
Function Buy tickets at the cinema

Vocabulary: Types of film

1a Listen and repeat. Then match the photos to the types of film.

Avatar – a science fiction film

- an action film • an animated film
- a comedy • a crime film
- a fantasy film • a horror film
- a musical • a romance
- a science fiction film • a spy film
- a thriller • a western

b Now write a film title for each type of film.

Read

2 Listen and read the Film File. What are Serena's favourite films?

Avatar

Mamma Mia!

Lord of the Rings

Skyfall

THE FILM FILE

This week Serena Martin lists her top three films of all time.

Number 1 — Men in Black

My FAVOURITE FILM OF ALL TIME: *Men in Black*. Will Smith and Tommy Lee Jones are in this film. Will Smith is a police officer **who** works with Agent K in Washington DC. The men work in a big office under the ground and their job is to find dangerous aliens. It's a great comedy film **which** has some scary moments, too.

Number 2 — Mean Girls

This film is a romance about a girl called Cady **who** goes to a new school. Here she meets a group of girls called the Plastics. They hang out at a café **where** she meets Aaron. She falls in love with him and her problems begin.

Number 3 — Toy Story 3

This is an animated film about a toy called Woody and his friends, Buzz Lightyear and Mr Potato Head. There's also a dog **which** bends, called Slinky Dog. The toys live in a school **where** children come and play with them. The kids aren't nice so Woody and his friends try to go back to their own home. It's an amazing film for all ages.

Comprehension

3 Answer the questions.

Which film …
1 is OK for young children to watch? *Toy Story 3*
2 is a love story?
3 is sometimes frightening?
4 has horrible children in it?
5 has a colour in the title?

Grammar

Defining relative clauses with *who*, *which* and *where*
People
This film is about a girl called Cady **who** goes to a new school.
Things
There's a dog **which** bends.
Places
They hang out at a café **where** she meets Aaron.

4 Read the Film File again. Notice the words in red.

Practice

5 Match (1–5) to (a–e). Then make sentences with *who*, *which* or *where*.

1 – c Agent K is a man who looks for aliens.

1 Agent K is a man
2 Cady goes to a school
3 This is a story
4 Washington DC is the city
5 There are some children

a) she meets the Plastics.
b) the Men in Black live.
c) looks for aliens.
d) are horrible to Woody.
e) makes you laugh.

6 Rewrite the story of *Night at the Museum* with *who*, *which* or *where*.

1 The story is about Larry Daley. He lives in New York.
   The story is about Larry Daley who lives in New York.

2 Every evening he goes to the Museum of Natural History. At the Museum of Natural History he works at night.

3 In the museum there are a lot of statues. They walk and talk every night.

4 There is also a magic tablet. It belongs to an Egyptian king.

5 Gus, Cecil and Reginald are bad men. They try and steal the tablet.

6 In the end Larry gets help from Roosevelt and Attila the Hun. They help him save the tablet.

Speak

7 Talk about you. Ask and answer.

1 What types of film do you like?
2 What's your favourite film?
3 What's it about?
4 Who's in it?

Write

8 Write about your favourite film.

My favourite film is …

Use your English: Buy tickets at the cinema

9 Listen and repeat. Then practise the conversation in pairs.

A: Can I have two teenage tickets for *The Hobbit*, please?
B: Which performance? The 6.45 or the 8.15?
A: The 6.45, please. How much is that?
B: That's £12, please.

Ask for tickets
Hello. I'd like/Can I have two teenage tickets for *The Hobbit*, please?
Ask about the performance
Which performance? The 6.45 or the 8.15?
Say the performance
The 6.45 performance, please.
Ask the price
How much is that?
Give the price
That's £12, please

10 Practise similar conversations. Use the film programme.

VISION CINEMA

Monsters University	1.30	5.30	
Grown Ups 2	4.15	6.00	8.30
Ender's Game	5.30	7.30	9.15
The Hobbit: The Desolation of Smaug	4.15	6.00	8.30

PRICES:
Adults: £8.50
Teenagers: £6.00
Under 12: £5.00
Book online at: www.vision.com/booking
Phone: 0208 576 45345 ☎

Extra practice

For more practice, go to page 55.

SKILLS FOCUS: READING

ACROSS **CULTURES**

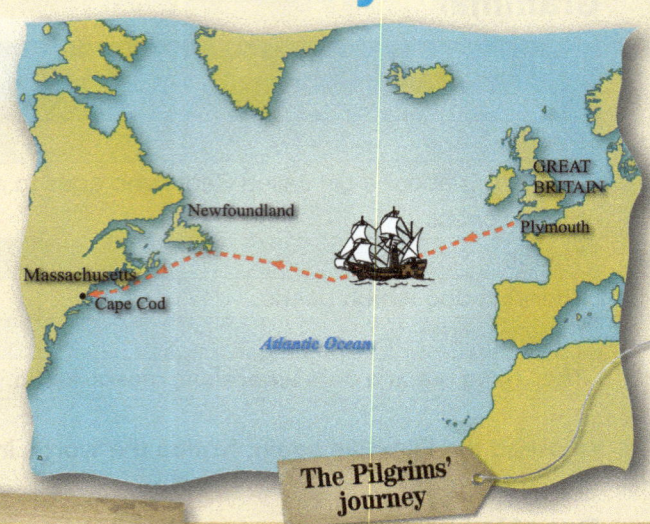

The Pilgrims' journey

Get started

1 Look at the pictures. Do you think journeys on this boat were easy? Why?/Why not?

Read

2 Read the story of the *Mayflower*. Who helped the Pilgrims when they arrived in America?

THE MAYFLOWER

The first English people travelled to America in 1620 on a ship called the *Mayflower*. There were 102 men, women and children on the ship. They are usually called 'the Pilgrims'. They left England because the king didn't like their religion.

The *Mayflower* was a very small boat for the journey of 4,500 kilometres. The ceiling was very low so some passengers couldn't stand up and there wasn't a toilet.

When they left the English port of Plymouth on 6th September 1620, it was good weather. But there were storms on the Atlantic Ocean and the waves were huge. A lot of the passengers and workers were seasick. One sailor and one passenger died.

After 66 days, the *Mayflower* arrived at Cape Cod, Massachusetts. It was winter and there was a lot of snow so the Pilgrims stayed on the ship until spring. There wasn't much food and it was very cold. A lot of them died. By spring only 53 passengers were still alive.

A Native American called Squanto from the Wampanoag tribe helped the Pilgrims. He taught them to catch fish and grow vegetables. He also showed them useful plants which were medicines.

In the summer of 1621, the Pilgrims harvested the food on their farms. In the autumn, the Pilgrims gave thanks for the harvest and they invited Squanto and his tribe to a meal. The Wampanoags brought a lot of food – turkey, fish, beans and berries. Today people in the USA have a holiday and a special meal every November on Thanksgiving Day. And they remember the Pilgrims who gave thanks for the harvest in 1621.

The Mayflower

Squanto

NEW WORDS
• king • religion • low • passengers
• port • storm • huge • seasick • sailor
• alive • Native American • tribe • catch
• grow • medicine • harvest (v)
• give thanks • turkey • berry/berries

READING TIP: GUESS MEANING FROM CONTEXT

When you find a new word in a text, don't stop reading. Try to guess the meaning from the context.

Now do Exercise 3.

3 **Complete the sentences with words from the New words box.**

1 _Passengers_ are people who travel on a boat, plane or train, for example.
2 Boats leave and arrive at a ___.
3 A ___ is a large bird. People eat it at Thanksgiving.
4 A ___ is like a family, but it's bigger.
5 ___ are small fruits.
6 When the rice in the fields is ready, the farmers ___ it.

Comprehension

4 **Choose the correct options.**

1 The Pilgrims left England because the king didn't like their
  a) language.
  b) ideas.
  c) children.

2 Life on the _Mayflower_ was
  a) difficult.
  b) comfortable.
  c) exciting.

3 The _Mayflower_ arrived at Cape Cod
  a) in the spring.
  b) in 1621.
  c) after 66 days.

4 When they got to Cape Cod,
  a) the Pilgrims immediately built a town.
  b) it was nearly summer.
  c) a lot of the Pilgrims died.

5 Squanto helped the Pilgrims
  a) to find food.
  b) to find wives.
  c) to meet other tribes.

6 By the summer of 1621,
  a) the Pilgrims were back in England.
  b) Squanto was very ill.
  c) the Pilgrims and the Wampanoags were friends.

Listen

5 **Listen and choose the correct options.**

1 Thanksgiving is in September / November.
2 It's on the fourth Tuesday / Thursday.
3 All offices / shops are closed on Thanksgiving Day.
4 People eat 46 / 56 million turkeys in the USA on Thanksgiving Day.
5 Thanksgiving Day became a holiday in 1853 / 1863.
6 President George Washington / Abraham Lincoln made it a holiday.

Speak

6 **Work in pairs. Roleplay a conversation with a tourist about a special meal in your country. Start like this:**

A: Do you have any special meals in your country?
B: Yes, we do on ... .
A: What things do you eat?
B: We start with ...

Project

7 **Write a paragraph for a tourist guidebook about a holiday in your country. Answer the questions.**

- When is it?
- Is there a special meal?
- How do people spend the day?
- What other things happen on this day?
- Do you know when this holiday started?

5e I always lose things.

Get ready to write

1 Read Jenny's story. What two things did she lose?

> I always lose things. Last year, on Thanksgiving Day, I was helping in the kitchen when I lost my favourite ring. I took it off to make an apple pie. A bit later, while we were all watching TV, I suddenly noticed my ring wasn't on my finger. I looked in the kitchen, but it wasn't there. At first I was really upset, but then I forgot about it. In the evening, we had our Thanksgiving meal. And guess what! My ring was in the apple pie! The next day I lost my earrings, but I didn't find them.

2 Read Jenny's story again and put the events in order. Number them 1–7.

- ☐ She found her ring in the pie.
- ☐ She made a dessert.
- ☐ She couldn't find her ring.
- ☐ 1 She took off her ring.
- ☐ She lost her earrings.
- ☐ They all watched TV.
- ☐ They sat down to eat.

WRITING TIP: TIME PHRASES *last week/ weekend/month/year, a bit/a minute later, suddenly, at first, then, in the morning/evening/afternoon, the next day*

In a story, use time words and phrases to link the events.

- *Last year*, on Thanksgiving Day, I was helping in the kitchen.
- *A bit later,* while we were all watching TV, I *suddenly* noticed my ring wasn't on my finger.
- *At first* I was really upset, but *then* I forgot about it.
- *In the evening*, we had our Thanksgiving meal.
- *The next day* I lost my earrings, but I didn't find them.

3 Read the story again. Circle the time phrases.

4 Complete the story with the phrases from the box.

> - At first • Then • The next day
> - in the evening • Last Saturday • suddenly

¹*Last Saturday* it was my mother's birthday so ²___ we went to a restaurant. After the meal my father couldn't find the car keys. ³___ he was calm and looked carefully in all his pockets. ⁴___ he got really worried. I had a good idea and ran back to the restaurant. I was asking the waiter about the keys when ⁵___ the chef came out of the kitchen with them. 'They're very clean,' he said, 'I found them in the dishwasher.' ⁶___, the restaurant sent my parents flowers and a card to say sorry.

Write

5 Write a story about the pictures called *Trouble at the beach*.

- Use time phrases.

Write 80–100 words.

Last weekend Julie, Rick and their dog, Shadow, went to the beach.

The next day

Grammar (15 marks)

1 Write sentences using **when** or **while** and the past continuous or past simple.

0 she/shop in town/lose her purse (while)
While she was shopping in town, she lost her purse.
00 I talk to Susanna/drop the phone on the floor
I was talking to Susanna when I dropped the phone on the floor.
1 he/watch a video/his mum phone (while)
2 I/stand/at the bus stop/a man take my purse (when)
3 they/live/in the USA/go to Disneyland (while)
4 We/play tennis/start to rain (when)
5 I/cycle home/have an accident (while)

.../10

2 Complete the sentences with **who**, **which** or **where**.

0 This is the town *where* I lived when I was a child.
1 Is there a shop near here ___ sells computers?
2 Can we find a place ___ we can sit down?
3 This is the girl ___ saw the accident.
4 Can you think of a name ___ begins with K?
5 That's the actor ___ was in *Dates*.

.../5

Vocabulary (17 marks)

3 Make adverbs from the adjectives in the box. Then complete the sentences.

• good • ~~loud~~ • angry • careful • hard
• quick

0 Please speak *loudly*. I can't hear you.
1 You've only got five minutes! Please write ___.
2 I always read the text ___ before I answer the questions.
3 Sally shouted ___ 'Go away'.
4 I'm sorry. I can't speak Spanish very ___.
5 Harry works very ___ at school.

.../5

4 Match the first half of a word in A to the second half in B to make types of film.

0 – e animated

A	*0 ani* 1 car 2 wes 3 hor 4 fan 5 thril
B	a) tern b) ror c) toon d) ler *e) mated* f) tasy

.../5

5 Write the correct preposition from the box.

• under • up • past • into • through
• over • ~~along~~ • down

0 *along* 1 2 3
4 5 6 7

.../7

Phrases/Use your English (8 marks)

6 Choose the correct response.

1 A: What was Peter doing at the toy shop?
  B: a) I expect he was buying his sister a present.
    b) I know he likes toys.
2 A: Guess what? You got an A in your Maths exam.
  B: a) You're winding me up!
    b) Certainly.
3 A: Is that your new tablet?
  B: a) No, it wasn't.
    b) Yes, have a look.
4 A: Are you sure it was Jess?
  B: a) Yes, honestly!
    b) Yes, all right.

.../4

7 Complete with a word from the box.

• performance, • Which • for • That's

A: Hello. I'd like two tickets [1]___ *The Hobbit*.
B: OK. [2]___ performance? The 6.15 or the 8.30?
A: The 6.15 [3]___ please. How much is that?
B: [4]___ £12 please.

.../4

LISTEN AND CHECK YOUR SCORE	
Grammar	.../15
Vocabulary	.../17
Phrases/Use your English	.../8
Total	**.../40**

6a The sea isn't warm enough.

Grammar *too* + adjective (+ infinitive)
(*not*) + adjective + *enough* (+ infinitive)

Vocabulary Places in town

Read

1 🎧 **6 01** **Listen and read the article. How long does it take to get from Brighton to London?**

MY HOME TOWN
Beautiful Brighton

I think Brighton is a wonderful place. It's got everything – theatres, cinemas, museums, lots of live music and a huge beach. OK, the waves aren't big enough to surf and the sea isn't warm enough for me. But, hey, on a sunny day you can sunbathe and put your toes in the water!

Brighton's most famous building is the Royal Pavilion. Until 1845, the royal family stayed in it when they visited Brighton. But now it's a museum. The Lanes are also very famous. They're little streets which are too small for cars. They're full of interesting shops, cafés and restaurants.

My cousins in London go to school by bus because it's too far to walk. But there are cycle paths here and it's safe enough to ride a bike. I'm not the only person who loves Brighton. It's full of tourists and students who come here to learn English. Why? Because it's a fun, friendly town which isn't very crowded and noisy, or very expensive. And it's close enough to London for a day trip. It's only an hour and a quarter by train.

✉ Adam, 17

Comprehension

2 **Answer true (T), false (F) or doesn't say (DS).**

1 There are lots of concerts in Brighton. *T*
2 Brighton is a long way from the sea.
3 The royal family sometimes stays in the Royal Pavilion.
4 You can't ride a bike in The Lanes.
5 There aren't many American tourists in Brighton.
6 There's a train station in Brighton.

Vocabulary: Places in town

3a **Recall Make a list of places in town. Then check the Word bank on page 59.**

b 🎧 02 **Extension** Listen and repeat. Then match seven place words from the box to the sentences (1–7). Which words have not got a sentence?

- art gallery • hospital • hotel • library
- market • museum • petrol station • police station
- shopping centre • theatre • travel agent
- tourist information centre • town hall • zoo

1 'I want to borrow a book.' *library*
2 'We want two plane tickets to New York.'
3 'I love looking at modern pictures.'
4 'Where can I buy fish, fruit and vegetables?'
5 'We're tourists here and we need a map and a list of hotels.'
6 'I'm interested in history. And I love old coins.'
7 'Help! My brother needs a doctor.'

4 Talk about places in your town.

We've got a flower market.   There isn't a theatre.

Grammar

too + adjective	(*not*) + adjective + *enough*
The streets are **too small** for cars.	The sea is**n't warm enough**.
too + adjective + infinitive	(*not*) + adjective + *enough* + infinitive
It's **too far to walk**.	It's **safe enough to ride** a bike.

5 Read the article again. Notice the words in red.

Practice

6 Use the notes and the correct adjectives to talk about Borington. Write sentences with *too* and *not ... enough*.

1 The cinema is too small./The cinema isn't big enough.

- small/big • noisy/quiet • dangerous/safe
- expensive/cheap • old/modern

Borington
1 cinema – only 50 seats
2 theatre – tickets cost £70
3 library – people talk there all the time
4 swimming pool – they built it in 1925!
5 streets – people drive very fast

7 Combine the sentences with *too ... to* or (*not*) ... *enough ... to*

1 He's very young. He can't go to the cinema on his own.
   He's too young to go to the cinema on his own.
2 It isn't warm. We can't have a picnic on the beach.
3 It's very noisy. We can't talk in this café.
4 It's very late. We can't go to the zoo.
5 The market isn't very near. Don't walk there.
6 It isn't very safe. Don't cycle on this street.

Speak

8 What is wrong with your town or village? Use adjectives from the box and your ideas.

- big • boring • cheap
- clean • comfortable • crowded
- dangerous • dirty • exciting
- expensive • far (from) • friendly
- interesting • modern
- near (to) • noisy • old • quiet
- safe • small

Our beach is too crowded.
The zoo isn't near enough to the centre.

Write

9 Write about your town. Use the questions to help you. Include two sentences with *too* and two sentences with (*not*) *enough*.

- Where do you live?
- What is there in your town/village?
- What are the good things about it?
- What are the bad things about it?
I live in Poznan in Poland …

Extra practice

For more practice, go to page 55.

15

Grammar Present continuous for future arrangements

Vocabulary Transport

Dialogue

1 🎧 **6 03 Listen and read. Complete the dialogue with the correct phrases.**

Kiran: What are you doing this weekend?

Jodie: I'm hanging out with my friend Nick from the Scilly Isles.

Kiran: The Scilly Isles! Where are they?

Jodie: They're miles away, off the coast of Cornwall.

Kiran: How's he getting here?

Jodie: ¹___ First he's taking a boat from St Agnes to St Mary's. Then he's getting a minibus to St Mary's airport. Then he's flying to Penzance.

Kiran: How's he getting from Penzance to London? Is he flying?

Jodie: No, he isn't. He's coming by train. It takes six hours.

Kiran: Wow! That's a long trip. When's he arriving?

Jodie: At seven on Thursday evening, ²___

Kiran: Are you meeting him at the station?

Jodie: Yes, I am. Then we're going home together. He thinks London's scary and he always gets lost on the Tube.

Kiran: ³___ how old is Nick?

Jodie: He's sixteen and he's very cool. But you know St Agnes is a really small island and there are only three cars on it.

Kiran: Three cars? ⁴___ That's really scary.

Phrases

- Remind me,
- It's complicated.
- I don't believe it!
- with a bit of luck.

Comprehension

2 **Answer the questions.**

1 Where does Nick live? *The Scilly Isles*

2 How old is he?

3 How many forms of transport is Nick going to use?

4 What does Nick think of London?

5 How many cars are there on St Agnes?

SOLVE IT!

3 **What time is Nick's train from Penzance?**

Vocabulary: Transport

4a Recall How many forms of transport can you write in half a minute? Check the Word bank on page 59.

b 🎧 04 **Extension** Listen and repeat. Then match the words to the photos (1–7).

- caravan • ferry • helicopter
- minibus • moped • ship • van

 1

 2

 3

 4

 5

 6

 7

Grammar

Present continuous for future arrangements

What **are** you **doing** this weekend?
I'm hanging out with Nick.
He**'s arriving** on Thursday.
Are you **meeting** him at the station?
Yes, I **am**.

5 Read the dialogue again. Notice the words in red.

Practice

6 Use the prompts to make Kiran's questions and Jodie's answers. Use the present continuous.

1 What are you doing on Friday?
2 In the morning we're going to Greenwich by boat. …

Kiran: ¹What/you/do/on Friday?
Jodie: ²In the morning/we/go to Greenwich by boat.³In the evening/we/meet my cousin.⁴She/take us to an Indian restaurant.
Kiran: ⁵Nick/go out with you/on Saturday?
Jodie: No. ⁶In the morning/I/go shopping, but Nick/not come with me.⁷He/go rollerblading with Tom.
Kiran: ⁸What/happen/on Sunday?
Jodie: ⁹Nick/leave.¹⁰He/not get the train because Alan/drive him to Penzance in his van.

Speak

7 In pairs, talk about their travel plans. Use the prompts. Then invent two more plans.

A: Where's Jack going?
B: He's going to a Scottish island.
A: How's he getting there?
B: He's going by coach and then by ferry.

Who?	Where to?	How?	
1 Jack	a Scottish island	coach	ferry
2 Julia	home	underground	taxi
3 Tim	a hotel in Venice	plane	boat
4 Sylvie and Sara	a holiday camp in France	train	minibus
5 You	?	?	?
6 My friend			

Extra practice

For more practice, go to page 55.

6c I'd like a green salad, please.

Grammar *Like* and *Would like*
Vocabulary Restaurant food
Function Order food in a restaurant

Dialogue

1 🎧 **6 05** **Listen and read. Which language is Tom practising and why?**

Emma: Oh, the menu says garlic prawns.
Tom: OK, what's the problem?
Emma: I like prawns, but I don't like garlic. Do you think …
Waiter: Hello. Are you ready to order?
Emma: I think so.
Waiter: What would you like?
Emma: Can I have the prawns without garlic, please?
Waiter: Yes, of course.
Emma: And, I'd like a green salad, please.
Waiter: And for you?
Tom: I'd like lasagne, please. No, sorry, ravioli.
Waiter: Ravioli. And would you like a salad?
Tom: Actually, I'd like spaghetti bolognese, not ravioli.
Waiter: Are you sure?
Tom: Yes, thanks, and a tomato salad. And can we have two colas, please?
Emma: That was embarrassing, Tom.
Tom: What was?
Emma: 'I'd like lasagne, sorry ravioli, actually spaghetti.' What's the matter with you?
Tom: I'm practising my Italian. We've got an Italian test next week.

Comprehension

2 **Choose the correct options.**

1 Emma orders **pasta / prawns** and a **tomato / green** salad.
2 Tom orders **ravioli / spaghetti** and a **tomato / green** salad.
3 Emma and Tom both want **juice / cola**.

Vocabulary: Restaurant food

3 🎧 **6 06** **Listen and repeat. Then write the words in the correct sections of the menu.**

- chips • garlic • fruit salad
- lemonade • prawns • ravioli
- roast chicken

Menu

Meat	
steak	£11.50
lamb kebab	£10.30
chicken curry	£8.50
1 _____	£9.75

Fish	
fish soup	£7.75
grilled sardines	£7.00
baked salmon	£9.50
2 _____	£8.50

Pasta	
spaghetti bolognese	£8.50
lasagne	£8.25
3 _____	£8.50

Pronunciation: /tʃ/ chicken, /ʃ/ fish

4 🎧 6 07 Go to page 60.

Grammar

Like and *Would like*
like
Do you **like** garlic prawns?   I **like** prawns, but I **don't like** garlic.
would like
I**'d like** spaghetti, please. (Can I have some … ?)   **Would** you **like** a salad?

5 Read the dialogue again. Notice the words in red.

Practice

6 Ask and answer about things to eat and drink.

- spaghetti • cheesecake • lamb kebab
- fruit juice • salad • ice cream • lemonade
- roast chicken • mashed potato

A: *Would you like some spaghetti?*
B: *Yes, please./No, thanks.*
A: *Do you like spaghetti?*
B: *Yes, I do. I love it./No, I don't. Not very much.*

Side orders (all at £3.95)
rice   fresh vegetables   green salad
tomato salad   garlic bread
baked potatoes   mashed potato
4 _____

Desserts (all at £5.75)
apple pie and cream
vanilla ice cream
chocolate ice cream
cheesecake
5 _____

Drinks (all at £2.50)
mineral water   fruit juice   cola
6 _____

There is a £3 cover charge per table

Listen

7 🎧 6 08 Listen and answer the questions.

1 What does Tom want for dessert?
2 What does Emma want?
3 How much is Tom's dessert?
4 How much is Emma's dessert?

SOLVE IT!

8 How much does Tom and Emma's meal cost altogether? Don't forget to add the cover charge!

Use your English: Order food in a restaurant

Ask what people want
Are you ready to order?   What would you like?   What would you like to drink?   Anything else?
Say what you want
I'd like spaghetti, please.   A chicken curry for me, please.   I'll have a lamb kebab, please.   Can I have a mineral water, please?   Me too, please.
Offer food or drink
Would you like some garlic bread?   With chips?
Accept or refuse
Yes, please./No, thank you.   Not for me, thanks.   No. That's fine, thanks.
Ask for the bill
Can I have the bill, please?

9 Roleplay conversations in a restaurant. Work in groups of three. Use the menu from Exercise 3 and order a full meal. Don't forget to work out the bill!

Extra practice

For more practice, go to page 56.

6d How honest are you?

REAL LIFE ISSUE

Get started

1 Put the actions in order: 1 = not very bad and 6 = very bad. Discuss your list.

A person …
a) ☐ steals £10 from a friend's jacket.
b) ☐ doesn't give back £10 to a friend who lent it.
c) ☐ says nothing when a shop assistant gives £10 extra change.
d) ☐ finds £10 in the street and keeps it.
e) ☐ says nothing when a waiter forgets to put things worth £10 on the bill.
f) ☐ steals things worth £10 from a shop.

Read

2 🎧 **8 09** Read the webpage and match Jenny and Robert's problems to actions (a–f) in Exercise 1.

Comprehension

3 Complete the sentences. Write *Sofia*, *Finn*, *Natalie* or *Gus*.

1 *Sofia* is worried about the person who lost the money.
2 ___ thinks it's a bad idea to take the money to the police station.
3 ___ knows a lot about the police from a parent.
4 ___ thinks it's a good idea to give the money to people who need it.
5 ___ had a job in a café or restaurant.
6 ___ felt good after she was honest.
7 ___ suggests a big tip.
8 ___ thinks the waiter wasn't good at his job.

www.talkandshare.com

TALK AND SHARE
Share your problems, share your solutions!

Search 🔍

Home | Forums | Contact Us

I found £20 in the street yesterday. It wasn't in a wallet. I want to keep it, but my sister Abby says I must take it to the police because that's the honest thing to do. I'm not sure. It's only £20.
Jenny

Your sister is too honest! Keep the money. How can the police find the owner? They're going to keep the money.
Finn

That's not true. My mother's in the police. She says that when they can't find the owner, they give the money to the person who found it. So I say – take the money to the police.
Natalie

Maybe the owner's very poor and saved that money for weeks. Put a notice in the street where you found the money AND take the money to the police.
Sofia

I think it's best to give the money to a charity for people who haven't got homes.   **Gus**

Speak your mind

4a First think about Jenny's problem. Who do you agree or disagree with, Sofia, Finn, Natalie or Gus? Give reasons.

I agree with Gus because the police don't always do the right thing.

b Now think about Robert's problem. Who do you agree or disagree with and why?

I disagree with Sofia ...

My problem's about money, too. I was at a café with a friend last week. The waiter forgot about our sandwiches and ice creams when he gave us the bill. So we just paid for our drinks. We saved £15!!! But I feel bad now. I think we were dishonest. **Robert**

Once a shop assistant gave me £20 change instead of £10. I noticed the mistake and told her. She was really happy and I felt good. Forget about the £15 this time. But don't do it again. **Sofia**

I think it was the waiter's fault. It's his job to give you a correct bill. Don't give the money back. **Finn**

I don't agree. I worked as a waitress last year. I got into trouble when I made mistakes like that. Write a note, put it with the money in an envelope and give it to the manager. **Natalie**

Go back to the café, order drinks from the same waiter and leave a big tip! **Gus**

Listen

5 Listen to Jenny's conversation with her sister and complete the summary.

1 Jenny took the money to the police station in *South* Street.
2 They asked her for her name, ___ and phone number.
3 She told them she found the money in ___ Road.
4 The police are going to keep the money for ___ days.
5 After the ___ it's too late for the owner to ask for the money.
6 Jenny isn't going to put a ___ about the money in the road.

SOLVE IT!

6 What is the date of Jenny and Abby's conversation in Exercise 5?

Write

7 Imagine Robert took Natalie's advice in Exercise 2. Write a note to the manager of the café. Say what happened, apologise and explain about the money in the envelope. Start like this:

My name's Robert Cardew. I was here with my friend last ... . We had ... , ... and ... .The bill was only ... because our waiter ... . I'm sorry we ... but here's the money now.
Best wishes
Robert

NEW WORDS
• keep (v) • honest • owner • poor
• save • notice • charity • dishonest
• fault • get into trouble • envelope • tip

21

Grammar (18 marks)

1 Write pairs of sentences with *too + adjective* and *not + adjective + enough*.

0 I can't do my homework here. It (quiet/noisy).
It isn't quiet enough. It's too noisy.

1 I've only got £20. Those trainers (expensive/cheap).

2 My little sister can't watch that scary film. She (young/old).

3 We can't cycle on that big road. It (safe/dangerous).

4 We can't swim in the lake. It (dirty/clean).

.../8

2 Complete with the correct form of the present continuous.

I'm really busy tomorrow. In the morning I ⁰'*m playing* (play) tennis. In the afternoon my brother Mark ¹___ (play) football for the school team so I ²___ (watch) him with Mum and Dad. In the evening Mark and I ³___ (make) the meal because it's Mother's Day. No, we ⁴___ (not have) pizza! We ⁵___ (cook) roast chicken!

.../5

3 Complete the dialogue with the correct form of *(not) like* or *would like*.

Dad: What ⁰*would* you *like* to eat?
John: I ¹___ some Italian food this evening.
Dad: What about pasta? You usually ²___ pasta.
John: Yes, but don't forget Mum ³___ it.
Dad: You're right. ⁴___ you ___ fish tonight?
Fern: No, thanks. You know John and I ⁵___ fish!

.../5

Vocabulary (13 marks)

4 Complete the word puzzle and find the hidden word.

	M	O	P	E	D
1	H				
2	C				
3	M				
4	F				
5	S				

.../5

5 Complete the places in town.

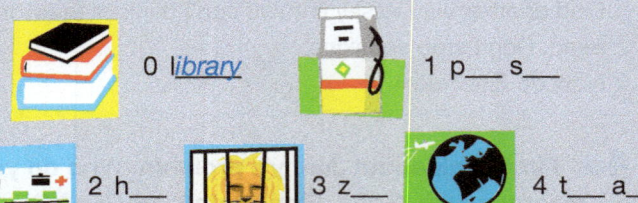

0 l*ibrary*

1 p___ s___

2 h___

3 z___

4 t___ a___

.../4

6 Match a word in A to a word in B to make a restaurant food phrase.

0 – d roast chicken

| A | 0 roast | 1 spaghetti | 2 garlic | 3 green | 4 apple |
| B | a) pie b) bread c) salad *d) chicken* e) bolognese | | | | |

.../4

Phrases/Use your English (9 marks)

7 Complete with phrases from the box.

- Remind me, • It's complicated.
- I don't believe it! • With a bit of luck,

1 A: Where's the nearest tube station?
B: ___ Have a look at this map on my smartphone.

2 A: Paul is arriving from New York today.
B: ___ how do you know him?

3 A: Don't forget we've got a test tomorrow.
B: ___ it's going to be easy!

4 A: My brother doesn't like computer games.
B: ___ That's really strange.

.../4

8 Look at the jumbled conversation. Number the lines in the correct order.

☐ a) And what would you like to drink?

[0] b) Are you ready to order?

☐ c) Can I have a mineral water, please?

☐ d) No, thank you.

☐ e) Would you like a green salad with that?

☐ f) Yes. I'd like lasagne, please.

.../5

🎧 6 11 LISTEN AND CHECK YOUR SCORE	
Grammar	.../18
Vocabulary	.../13
Phrases/Use your English	.../9
Total	**.../40**

Skills Revision

Read

1 **Read the text and choose the correct options.**

The cinema was born on 28th December 1895. On that day, for the first time, people paid to watch films. The film-makers were brothers – Auguste and Louis Lumière. The **audience** watched ten short films in the basement of a Paris café.

One film was called *Fishing For* **Goldfish**. A man holds a baby near a **bowl** with water and goldfish in it. The baby puts his hand in the water and tries to get the fish. *Water On The Waterer* is the world's first comedy. A gardener is **watering** plants. A boy stands on the **hose** and the water stops. The gardener doesn't see the boy so he looks at the end of the hose to check it. At that moment the boy takes his foot off the hose and the water goes on the gardener's face. This film is 49 **seconds** long.

Louis Lumière didn't believe in his invention. He said 'The cinema hasn't got a future. People prefer to watch life in the real world, in the street.' He was wrong, of course.

0 Auguste and Louis Lumière
   a) were born in 1895.
   b) were brothers.
   c) had a café.
1 People watched
   a) 10 films in the first film show.
   b) 20 films in the first film show.
   c) films for free in a Paris café.
2 In *Fishing For Goldfish*
   a) a man goes fishing.
   b) a baby falls in the water.
   c) a baby's hand gets wet.
3 The Lumières also made a film about
   a) a man who gets very wet.
   b) a man who hurts his face.
   c) a boy who doesn't like gardens.
4 Louis Lumière's opinion about the cinema was
   a) 'It's got a great future.'
   b) 'It isn't going to be popular.'
   c) 'We need one on every street.'

2 **Read the text again and try to understand the meaning of the underlined words. Then translate them into your language.**

Listen

3 🎧 **Listen to six friends ordering food online. What does each person want for their main course? Write a letter (A–H) next to each person. There are two extra main courses.**

0 Elaine   [H]
1 Celia   ☐
2 Mitch   ☐
3 Ruby   ☐
4 Daisy   ☐
5 Scott   ☐

A baked salmon
B fish soup
C garlic prawns
D grilled chicken
E grilled sardines
F lamb kebab
G lasagne
H pizza

Write

4 **Write a short story about a complicated journey. Use the questions to help you. Write 80–100 words.**

• When was this journey?
• Where were you travelling from and to?
• Why were you going there?
• Were you alone? Who were you with?
• How many different forms of transport did you use?
• What time did the journey start?
• How long did the journey take?
• What was the first form of transport? Then ... ? And after that ...?
• Were there any problems on the journey? (Did you get up late?/miss the bus/train?/lose your ticket/passport/money/luggage?)
• What time did you finally arrive?
• Who met you at the end of your trip?
• How did you feel at the end of the trip?

Start like this:
I went on a really complicated journey last .../... ago.

NOW I CAN	
Read	understand a short text about the cinema and find specific information. ☐
Listen	understand the main message in a simple conversation about food. ☐
Write	write a short story about a journey. ☐

7 HAVING FUN!

Grammar	Present perfect simple with *ever*, *never*
	The definite article with places
Vocabulary	Holiday activities

Vocabulary: Holiday activities

1 Recall List as many holiday activities as you can. Put them in four groups. Then check the Word bank on page 59.

- in the sea: *go swimming/swim*
- on the beach:
- in the mountains:
- in town:

Read

2 Listen and read Ted's Travel Blog. Who is Kirsty jealous of?

TED'S TRAVEL BLOG

This week Ted gives one reader some ideas for an unusual winter holiday.

Hi Ted,
I've had a lot of great summer holidays in the USA with my family. We've been mountain biking in the Rockies, I've played beach volleyball on a sports holiday and I've windsurfed in Florida. But I'm jealous of my friend, Paul, in France. He's never been windsurfing, but he's been snowboarding and skiing in the Alps. And he's seen a bear in the snow. I haven't!
I've never tried any winter sports. I'd like a winter holiday this year. Where can we go?

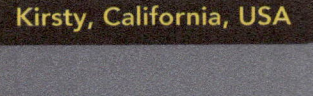

Kirsty, California, USA

Comprehension

3 Answer the questions.

1 What did Kirsty do on a sports holiday?
   beach volleyball
2 Where does Paul live?
3 What type of holiday does Kirsty want?
4 What country does Ted suggest?
5 What activities can you do there?

Note

The definite article with places
We use the definite article with the following:
- plural countries   • mountains   • rivers
- seas and oceans   • groups of islands   • deserts
(the USA, the Alps, the Rockies)

Hi Kirsty,
Wow! You've done a lot of interesting things. But I agree – winter holidays can be amazing. Have you ever been to Canada? It's a great place for winter sports. Have you ever ridden a snowmobile? Have you ever tried dog sledding? Well, you can do both those things in Alberta, Canada.

Have fun and don't forget to pack your warmest clothes!
Ted

Grammar

Present perfect simple with *ever, never*	
Affirmative	**Negative**
I**'ve played** beach volleyball. He**'s seen** a bear in the snow. We**'ve been** mountain biking.	I**'ve never tried** any winter sports. He**'s never been** windsurfing. We**'ve never had** a winter holiday.
Yes/No questions	Short form
Have you **ever been** to Canada? **Has** he **ever played** beach volleyball? **Have** we **ever ridden** a snowmobile?	Yes, I **have.**/No, I **haven't.** Yes, he **has.**/No, he **hasn't.** Yes, we **have.**/No, we **haven't.**

The present perfect uses the past participle of the verb. Turn to page 64 for a list of irregular past participles.

➤ Now make sentences with *she* and *they*.

4 Read the travel tips again. Notice the words in red.

> **Note**
>
> The verb *go* has two past participles:
> They've gone to Canada. = They went to Canada and they are still there.
> They've been to Canada. = They went to Canada, but they are now back home.

Practice

5 Complete the dialogue.

Emma: Look at this quiz in my magazine. It asks 'What ¹*have you done* (you/do)?' and 'What ²___ (you/never/do)?'

Tom: OK, so ³___ (you/ever/try) windsurfing?

Emma: No, I haven't. And ⁴___ (I/never/play) beach volleyball. ⁵___ (you/ever/see) a judo competition?

Tom: Yes, I have. I saw one last year.

Emma: ⁶___ (you/ever/eat) Japanese food?

Tom: No, I haven't and ⁷___ (I/never/drink) green tea, but I'd like to try it.

Emma: Me, too. OK, next question, ⁸___ (you/ever/climb) a mountain?

Tom: No, and ⁹___ (I/never/try) dog sledding.

Emma: Ah, I know the answer to this question. ¹⁰___ (you/ever/sing) in a show?

Tom: Yes, I have!!

Speak

6a Ask and answer.

1 go
A: *Have you ever been to Paris?*
B: *Yes, I have./No, I haven't.*

go

eat

ride

sleep

see

go

b Tell the class about your partner.

Ewa's been to Paris but she's never …

Write

7 Write to a friend who is coming to stay with you for a week.

- Think of three interesting things to do or see and ask if your friend has ever done or seen them.
- Tell your friend about one thing you have never done and ask if he or she would like to do this.

Hi Colette,
It's great you're coming to stay with me. Have you ever seen/been/tried … ?

Extra practice

For more practice, go to page 56.

Grammar Present perfect with *just*, *already* and *yet*
Function Exclamations

Emma: **Have** you **bought** Jodie's birthday present **yet**?
Tom: **I've ordered** a DVD online, but it **hasn't arrived yet**.
Emma: But her birthday's tomorrow!
Tom: I know. **I've just spent** an hour on the phone to them.
Emma: An hour! What a nightmare!
Tom: ¹___ they say they'**ve already sent** the DVD, but it's going to arrive next week.
Emma: That's a shame! It's going to be late.
Tom: Well, **I've done** my best. Anyway where's your present for her?
Emma: Look, it's a bracelet. ²___
Tom: Wow! Where's it from?
Emma: **I've just made** it.
Tom: ³___ you'**ve just bought** it!
Emma: No, honestly.
Tom: That's amazing! Can you say it's from me, too?
Emma: No way!
Tom: OK, ⁴___ I was only joking.

Phrases
- You mean
- calm down.
- The trouble is,
- What do you reckon?

Dialogue

1 🎧 **7 02** **Listen and read the dialogue. Complete with the correct phrases.**

Comprehension

2 Answer true (T), false (F) or doesn't say (DS).

1 Tom wants to give Jodie a DVD. *T*
2 Tom bought Jodie's present in a shop.
3 Tom's present is going to arrive early.
4 Emma likes making earrings.
5 Tom thinks Emma's present is great.

Grammar

Present perfect with *just*, *already* and *yet*	
Affirmative	**Negative**
I**'ve just made** it. They**'ve already sent** the book.	I haven't bought it **yet**. It hasn't arrived **yet**.
Yes/No questions	Short answers
Have you bought a present **yet**?	Yes, I **have**. No, I **haven't**.

➤ **Now make sentences with *you*, *he* and *they*.**

3 **Read the dialogue again. Notice the words in red.**

SOLVE IT!

4 **What date is Jodie's birthday?**

Practice

5 **Complete the dialogues using the prompts and *just*, *yet* or *already*.**

1 **A:** ¹*Have you started your homework yet* (you/start/homework)?
B: Yes, ²___ (I/finish/it). I did it two hours ago.
A: Can you help me? I can't do mine.

2 **A:** ³___ (you/buy/the new *Angry Birds* game)?
B: No, ⁴___ (I/not see/it). Is it good?
A: It's awesome! ⁵___ (I/play/30 games) with my brother.

3 **A:** ⁶___ (you/have/your English exam results)?
B: Yes, ⁷___ (I/speak/to Mrs Jones). I got 90%.
A: That's brilliant. ⁸___ (I/not see/her). I'm a bit worried.

Pronunciation: /ʊ/ b**oo**k, /uː/ y**ou**

6 🎧 7/03 **Go to page 60.**

Use your English: Exclamations

7 🎧 7/04 **Listen and repeat. Then practise the conversation in pairs.**

A: I've just lost my purse.
B: That's awful!
A: Luckily there isn't any money in it.
B: That's good!

	Surprise What a surprise! How strange/weird! That's odd! No way! You're joking! That's incredible!
	Pleasure That's good/great! How amazing/nice! What a fantastic present/ show/evening!
	Horror What a nightmare! How horrible/disgusting! That's awful!
	Disappointment What a pity! That's a pity! That's a shame!

8 **Practise similar conversations with the prompts. Use *Luckily* or *Unfortunately*.**

1 My mum/win/the lottery (she/can't find the ticket)
  A: My mum has just won the lottery.
  B: How amazing!
  A: Unfortunately, she can't find the ticket.
  B: That's awful.
2 My sister/fall off bike (she/OK)
3 I/win/a meal for four at the Chinese restaurant (I/not like/Chinese food)
4 My brother/had/an accident (he/not hurt)
5 I/drop/my MP3 player (it/OK)

Extra practice

For more practice, go to page 56.

Grammar   Past simple and present perfect simple
Vocabulary   Types of music

Vocabulary: Types of music

1a   Recall Write all the different types of music you can remember. Check the Word bank on page 59.

b   Can you think of one musician for each type of music?

Read

2   🎧 7 05   Listen and read the article. How many people want to go on *The X Factor* each year?

WHAT IS THE FACTOR?

Have you ever seen *The X Factor*? It's the biggest talent show in Europe and every year millions of people audition for it. The show has made a lot of people famous. Simon Cowell started the show in 2004. There are four judges. They listen to the singers, choose their favourites and help them with their music. Almost ten million people in the UK watch the show on TV.

The first winner was Steve Brookstein in 2004. He sang a rock song on *The X Factor*, but he has never had a big hit and now he sings jazz in small clubs. Another winner was Leona Lewis. She won the show in 2006 and has already sold more than twenty million records.

Sometimes the losers do better than the winners. Olly Murs came second on the show in 2009 and the boy band, One Direction, finished third in 2010. Olly and One Direction have already become very famous and have fans all over the world. So maybe it's better NOT to win!

Comprehension

3 **Choose the correct options.**

1 *The X Factor* is for
   a) famous singers.   b) new singers.

2 The judges
   a) sing on the show. b) help the singers.

3 Steve Brookstein now sings
   a) jazz.   b) rock.

4 Leona Lewis won in
   a) 2006.   b) 2010.

5 In 2010, One Direction
   a) won.   b) came third.

SOLVE IT!

4 **How many winners were there before Leona Lewis?**

Grammar

Past simple and present perfect simple
Past simple
Simon Cowell **started** the show in 2004.
Present perfect simple
Leona Lewis **has already sold** more than twenty million records.

5 **Read the article again. Notice the words in red.**

Practice

6 **Write questions and sentences. Use the past simple or the present perfect simple.**

1 I/go/a rock concert/yesterday
   I went to a rock concert yesterday.

2 Laura/never/watch/a musical
   Laura has never watched a musical.

3 you/ever/see/a rap artist?

4 Zak/write/a song last month?

5 Pete/just/meet/Bruno Mars

6 My mum/buy/her MP3 player in 2009

---

7 **Complete the dialogue with the past simple or present perfect simple.**

Jonas: Hi, Ellie. Where ¹*have you been* (be)?

Ellie: I ²___ (just/have) an audition for *The X Factor*.

Jonas: Wow! What song ³___ (you/sing)?

Ellie: I ⁴___ (sing) *Rolling in the Deep*.

Jonas: I ⁵___ (never/hear) of it. Who ⁶___ (write) it?

Ellie: It's by Adele. It's quite an old song.

Jonas: Oh. ⁷___ (see) Simon Cowell at the audition?

Ellie: No, he ⁸___ (not/be) there.

Listen

8 🎧 **Listen to Matt and Alice talking about a *Wow Factor!* audition. Choose the correct options.**

1 What did Matt sing?
   a) You're in my head
   b) You're in my heart
   c) You're in my house

2 What kind of song is it?
   a) a love song
   b) a sad song
   c) a new song

3 Who did he meet?
   a) Rod Stewart
   b) Steven Powell
   c) Mark Harlow

4 What did the judge do? He
   a) sang the song.
   b) helped the singers.
   c) left early.

5 When is the next audition?
   a) today
   b) tomorrow
   c) next week

Speak

9 **Talk about you. Ask and answer with a friend. Use your imagination.**

1 be/a music festival? (When/go? Where/go?)
   A: Have you ever been to a music festival?
   B: Yes, I have.
   A: When did you go?
   B: I went last summer?
   A: Where did you go?
   B: I went to Reading festival. It was great.

2 win/a talent show? (What/do? What/win?)

3 buy/a music DVD? (What/buy? How much/cost?)

4 meet/a famous person? (Who/meet? What/say?)

5 be/an opera? (What/see? Who/go with?)

Extra practice

For more practice, go to page 56.

SKILLS FOCUS: READING

ACROSS **CULTURES**

Cornwall

Have you ever been to Cornwall in the south-west of Britain? It's one of the UK's most popular places for holidays. It has old fishing villages, beautiful beaches, excellent surfing, delicious Cornish ice cream and the best weather in the country.

The top things to do on holiday here:

- See a play at the Minack Theatre. It's like a Roman theatre, without walls or a roof and it has fantastic views of the sea.
- Enjoy the fabulous paintings and sculptures at the Tate Gallery in St Ives.
- Visit the Seal Sanctuary, a home for baby seals. When they lose their parents in stormy weather at sea, they live here in a big salt water swimming pool. They're really sweet with their big black eyes!
- Eat fish in Mousehole. It's one of the prettiest villages in Cornwall.
- Go surfing at Porthcurno Beach. There are fifteen kilometres of golden sand and giant waves.

The Minack Theatre

Fishing boats in Mousehole

Florida

People call Florida 'the sunshine state' because it has the warmest weather in the USA. It's in the south-east and it's a great place for a holiday!

Five things to do in Florida:

1 Visit the Everglades and travel through mangrove forests in a boat. But you can't swim here. There are alligators in the water.
2 Go to St Augustine, the oldest city in the USA. Spanish people built it in 1565. It's got old Spanish houses, a famous castle and some beautiful beaches.
3 See the Florida Keys. Go snorkelling or scuba diving around these islands and see thousands of multi-coloured fish. Watch dolphins. They love jumping and playing in the water.
4 Learn about space at the Kennedy Space Centre. You can see real spaceships and meet astronauts.
5 Spend time in Miami. South Beach is famous, but look at the buildings, too. There are a lot of amazing skyscrapers. Some of them are 120 metres high.

Scuba diving in the Florida Keys

Alligators in the Everglades

NEW WORDS
- fishing village
- without
- fabulous
- painting
- seal
- stormy
- giant
- mangrove
- alligator
- go snorkelling
- go scuba diving
- multi-coloured
- dolphin
- skyscraper

Get started

1 Look at the photos. Which place would you like to visit in your holidays? Why?

Read

2 (7.07) Read the holiday guides. Find the name of a beach in Cornwall and a beach in Florida.

> **READING TIP: WORK OUT MEANINGS**
>
> - Some words are like words you already know. For example, *fishing* and *stormy* are like *fish* and *storm*.
> - Guess the meaning from context. For example, *Go surfing at Porthcurno; there are ... giant waves*. You can guess *giant* means *big* because small waves aren't good for surfing.
> - Guess the meaning from a picture and the words under it. For example, *Alligators in the Everglades*.
> - Guess the general meaning. For example, *mangrove* is a tree because there are *mangrove forests*.

3 Find the words in the New words box with these meanings.

1 a very tall building *skyscraper*
2 very windy ___
3 three types of animal (not fish) in the water ___, ___, ___
4 with lots of different colours ___
5 in this place a lot of people catch fish as a job ___

Comprehension

4 Match the place names to the descriptions (1–7).

> - The Minack • The Tate • Mousehole
> - Porthcurno • St Augustine • The Keys • Miami

1 a very old town in Florida *St Augustine*
2 a beach ___
3 a fishing village ___
4 a group of islands ___
5 a modern city ___
6 a gallery ___
7 a theatre ___

Listening

5 (7.08) Listen and choose the correct options.

1 The Minack Theatre is
   a) Greek.   b) Roman.   c) 80 years old.

2 Minack comes from the Cornish word
   a) MEINEK.   b) MEYNEK.   c) MIYNEK.

3 The last Cornish speaker died in
   a) 1777.   b) 1770.   c) 1707.

4 The word tempest means
   a) a rock.   b) a storm.   c) a view.

5 You can't see plays at the Minack in
   a) April.   b) July.   c) September.

Speak

6 Practise the conversation in pairs. Then change the words in red and practise it again.

A: I've just got back from Cornwall.
B: I've never been there. What's it like?
A: It's got the best weather in the UK.
B: What did you do there?
A: I saw a play at the Minack Theatre.
B: That sounds interesting. What other things can you do there?
A: You can go surfing at Porthcurno Beach.

Project

7 Write a holiday guide about a popular area in your country.

- What's the area called?
- Where is it?
- What's the weather like there?
- What's it famous for?
- Suggest some things to do, see, visit, learn about, buy or eat there.

This is a photo of Mousehole in Cornwall.

SKILLS FOCUS: WRITING AN INVITATION

Get ready to write

1 Read the email. When is Eleanor going on holiday?

Hi Claire,

We're going to spend August in Cornwall. My grandparents have got a house there. It's got great views of the sea. Would you like to come and stay?

The house is very near the beach. We can cycle there. There's a group of really nice surfers at the beach. I made friends with them last year.

You can come any time in August. In fact, you can come with us from London by car on 2nd August, but the drive is quite long and boring! Or you can get the train to Penzance. What do you think?

Love from
Eleanor

2 Correct the sentences.

1 Eleanor has got a house in Cornwall.
2 You can see the town from the house.
3 You can get to the beach by train.
4 Eleanor's friends are horse riders.
5 Eleanor's family is flying to Cornwall

WRITING TIP: ADDING EXTRA DETAILS

We can make our writing more interesting when we give extra information.

a) *My grandparents have got a house there.*
   Extra detail: *It's got great views of the sea.*
b) *The house is very near the beach.*
   Extra detail: *We can cycle there.*
c) *There's a group of really nice surfers at the beach.*
   Extra detail: *I made friends with them last year.*
d) *You can come with us from London by car on 2nd August,*
   Extra detail: *but the drive is quite long and boring!*

3 Match another extra detail below to each sentence in the tip box.

1 I really like one guy called Matt. ___
2 It takes about five hours. ___
3 And it's got apple trees in the garden. ___
4 There's a cycle path through the fields. ___

4 Read the email and complete it with the extra details (a–e).

Hi George,
My aunt and uncle have moved to Paris. ¹<u>e</u>
They've invited me and a friend to stay the last week of July. Would you like to come? We can visit the Louvre Museum. ²___ And we can hire bikes. ³___ And I want to be a typical tourist and go up the Eiffel Tower. ⁴___ We can also go to cafés. ⁵___
Bye for now!
Simon

Extra details

a) And we can order our food in French!
b) It's a great way to see the city.
c) It's full of famous paintings and sculptures.
d) The view from the top is amazing.
e) They've got a big flat in the centre.

Write

5 Write an email to a friend.

- Invite him/her to come with you on a camping trip.
- Answer these questions and add extra details where possible.

a) In which country/area are you going camping?
b) When are you going and how long for?
c) What's the campsite like?
d) Who are you going with?
e) How are you travelling?
f) What are you going to do there?

Language Revision

Grammar (20 marks)

1 **Complete with the present perfect simple.**

A: 0*Have you ever been* (you/ever/be) snowboarding?

B: Yes, I have. But 1___ (I/never/try) skiing.

A: 2___ (you/ever/ride) a snowmobile?

B: No, I haven't. But 3___ (I/see) a bear.

A: 4___ (you/ever/do) anything scary?

B: Well, 5___ (I/be) dog sledding. That was scary!

.../5

2 **Complete in the present perfect. Use a verb from the box and just, already or yet.**

- not speak - get up - win - ~~not see~~
- leave - start

0 I *haven't seen* Skyfall *yet*. (yet)

1 The concert ___. In fact, it started an hour ago. (already)

2 The new boy's called Alex. I ___ to him ___. (yet)

3 Murray ___ ten matches this year. (already)

4 Jodie ___ for school. She left a minute ago. (just)

5 It's 9 o'clock. ___ Sam ___? (yet)

.../5

3 **Complete with the present perfect or past simple.**

Thank you for the money. It 0*arrived* (arrive) last week and I 1___ (already/spend) it! Holly and I 2___ (go) shopping and I 3___ (buy) a new MP3 player. I 4___ (never/have) an MP3 player before. I 5___ (already/download) some songs onto it. Mum 6___ (just/come) back from Paris. She 7___ (have) a great time and the weather 8___ (be) great. 9___ (be) your holiday nice? We 10___ (not/have) our holiday yet.

.../10

Vocabulary (12 marks)

4 **Match the holiday activities to the people.**

- go shopping - go climbing
- ~~go skiing~~ - go to a musuem

0 Jake: I fell in the snow a lot. *go skiing*

1 Dom: I went to the top of a mountain.

2 Alice: I saw interesting old coins.

3 Katy: I bought some new clothes.

.../3

5 **Rearrange the letters to make types of music.**

0 iph-ohp   *hip-hop*

1 natil ___	4 lofk ___	7 ppo ___
2 thonec ___	5 islslcaca ___	8 par ___
3 eeggar ___	6 uosl ___	9 zajz ___

.../9

Phrases/Use your English (8 marks)

6 **Complete with phrases from the box.**

- You mean - the trouble is, - calm down.
- What do you reckon?

1 **A:** Please stop shouting and ___

   B: OK, OK.

2 **A:** Look, I've just made a cake for Harry.

   B: ___ you bought it! You hate cooking!

3 **A:** Have you bought a new camera yet?

   B: Yes, but ___ it doesn't work.

4 **A:** Is that a new shirt?

   B: Yes. ___

   A: I really like it.

.../4

7 **Choose the correct response.**

0 **A:** Max has won £5,000 on the lottery.

   B: a) That's amazing!   b) That's a shame!

1 **A:** My brother's just had an accident.

   B: Oh, no!   a) That's great.   b) How horrible!

2 **A:** My sister's failed her driving test.

   B: a) That's a shame!   b) How weird.

3 **A:** I've just found my MP3 player in the fridge!

   B: a) How odd!   b) What a pity!

4 **A:** I lost my purse in town this afternoon.

   B: a) How nice.   b) What a nightmare!

.../4

7 09	**LISTEN AND CHECK YOUR SCORE**	
Grammar		.../20
Vocabulary		.../12
Phrases/Use your English		.../8
Total		.../40

Grammar   Zero conditional with *if*
Vocabulary   Personality adjectives

8 JUST IMAGINE

Are you a wolf or a lamb?

Some people are wolves. If they want things, they take them and they don't worry about other people. And some people are lambs. They're generous, polite and helpful. Which are you?

1 **If I go to a café with friends, I …**
   a) leave my purse at home.
   b) pay for my drink only.
   c) pay for everyone.

2 **If an older person needs a seat on the bus, I …**
   a) look out of the window.
   b) wait five minutes then offer my seat.
   c) stand up immediately.

3 **If a friend needs to borrow money, I …**
   a) say 'I haven't got any'.
   b) lend him fifty pence.
   c) give him five pounds.

4 **If my friend doesn't understand her homework, I …**
   a) turn on the television.
   b) help her for exactly five minutes.
   c) help her for an hour.

5 **If my friend's hungry, I …**
   a) say 'Bad luck!'
   b) give her three crisps.
   c) buy her a sandwich.

Key
Mostly a's Why are you so mean and rude, you horrible wolf?
Mostly b's You're half wolf and half lamb. Try to be kinder.
Mostly c's You're a generous, friendly lamb! Everyone loves you.

Read

1 🎧 **Listen and read and do the quiz. Then read the key.**
   Are you a wolf, a lamb or a mixture?

34

Vocabulary: Personality adjectives

2 🎧 8 02 **Listen and repeat. Write the words in two lists, positive and negative. Which two adjectives aren't positive or negative?**

Positive	Negative
clever	*annoying*

- annoying • bad-tempered • big-headed
- bossy • clever • cute • easy-going
- friendly • funny • generous • hard-working
- helpful • honest • kind • lazy • loyal
- mean • polite • quiet • rude • shy • tidy
- unfriendly • untidy

Listen

3 🎧 8 03 **Read the list of adjectives. Then listen and match the speakers to the adjectives.**

- ☐ polite
- 1 big-headed
- ☐ bossy
- ☐ generous
- ☐ hard-working
- ☐ honest
- ☐ lazy
- ☐ mean

Write

4 **What do you think? Complete the sentences with adjectives from the box in Exercise 2.**

1 I like *friendly and funny* people.
2 I don't like ___ people.
3 My best friend is ___.
4 One of my friends is sometimes a bit ___.
5 I try to be ___.
6 Sometimes I'm a bit ___, but I try not to be.
7 The best thing about me is I'm ___.

Grammar

Zero conditional with *if*

If an older person **needs** a seat on the bus, I **stand up** immediately.
If my friend **doesn't understand** her homework, I **help** her for an hour.
What **do** you **do if** a friend **wants** to borrow money?

5 **Read the quiz again. Notice the words in red.**

Practice

6 **Write sentences with *if* and the present tense.**

1 people (be) late/I (get) annoyed with them
   If people are late, I get annoyed with them.
2 my sister (want) to borrow my clothes/she always (ask) me first
3 my little brother (not want) to go to bed/he (start) crying
4 a DVD (make) me laugh/I (watch) it again
5 my mother (not like) a film/I usually (like) it!

7 **Match (1–6) to (a–f) and make sentences with *if*.**

1 – f If there's a scary bit in a film, I usually shut my eyes.

1 there (be) a scary bit in a film
2 my friend (get) top marks in a test
3 my friend (not have got) any money for the cinema
4 I (wake) up early at the weekend
5 I (feel) a bit sad
6 I (not eat) breakfast

a) I always feel hungry by ten.
b) I sometimes pay for her.
c) I go back to sleep.
d) I watch a funny DVD and then I feel better.
e) I sometimes feel a bit jealous.
f) I usually shut my eyes.

Speak

8 **Choose three sentence beginnings from Exercise 7. Write different endings to make them true for you. Then tell the class.**

If there's a scary bit in a film, I usually scream.

Extra practice

For more practice, go to page 57.

Grammar *Will* for future predictions
Vocabulary The weather

Read

1 🎧 8/04 Listen and read the competition entries. Which year in the future is the competition about?

COMPETITION:
FUTURE WORLD

We asked: One hundred years from now what will the world be like? Will life be different?

THESE ARE THE WINNERS:

My picture shows the Earth 100 years from now. It will rain a lot and there won't be any deserts. It won't snow in the Arctic – it will be warm and sunny there. The oceans will be bigger and it will be dangerous to live near the sea. All cities will be on mountains. People will have boats and bicycles. They won't travel by car or plane.

Natasha (15)

In 100 years' time, the world will be very hot and windy and there won't be many lakes or rivers. As you see in my picture, there will be huge deserts. Antarctica will have the biggest cities, but people will also live on Mars. We'll have electric cars and planes and we'll get all our energy from the sun and wind. Robots will do all our work. Everyone will live to the age of 150 so I'll still be here!

Justin (16)

Comprehension

2 Who writes about these topics? Tick (✓) the boxes.

Topics	Natasha	Justin
1 boats and bicycles	✓	
2 cars and planes		
3 cities		
4 deserts		
5 lakes and rivers		
6 Mars		
7 oceans		
8 robots		

Grammar

Will for future predictions	
Affirmative	**Negative**
It **will rain** a lot.	It **won't** (**will not**) **snow** in the Arctic.
Yes/No **questions**	**Short answers**
Will life **be** different?	Yes, it **will**./No, it **won't**.

3 Read the competition entries again. Notice the words in red.

Practice

4 What do the texts say about the topics in Exercise 2?

People will have boats and bicycles.

5 Complete the Future World competition entry with *will*, *'ll* or *won't* and the verb in brackets.

In the twenty-second century, the Earth ¹*will be* (be) a very hot place. People ²___ (wear) special clothes to stay cool and they ³___ (not/go) outside very often. They ⁴___ (fly) everywhere in little spacecars. How ⁵___ they ___ (get) their food? Well, people ⁶___ (not eat) real food. They ⁷___ (take) special pills instead. And sick people ⁸___ (buy) new body parts from special body banks. Who ⁹___ (do) all the work? Robots, of course. People ¹⁰___ (not do) any work.

Vocabulary: The weather

6a **Recall** What is the weather like in the pictures? Say other weather words. Then check the Word bank on page 59.

1 It's sunny./The sun's shining.

b In your country what is the weather usually like: in January? in April? in July? in October? on your birthday?

It's usually cold here in January. It rains a lot.

Speak

7 Ask and answer questions about the weather around the world tomorrow.

A: What will the weather be like in Paris tomorrow?
B: It will be foggy and it will be cold.

TOMORROW'S WEATHER AROUND THE WORLD

CITY	WEATHER	TEMPERATURE
1 Paris	foggy	7°C
2 Cairo	sunny	20°C
3 Rome	windy	11°C
4 Brasilia	sunny	34°C
5 Oslo	cloudy	-10°C
6 Sydney	rain	26°C
7 Warsaw	snow	-5°C

S☺LVE IT!

8 What is the difference in temperature between the hottest and the coldest places on the weather chart in Exercise 7?

Pronunciation: /aʊ/ n<u>ow</u>, /əʊ/ sn<u>ow</u>

9 🎧 8/05 Go to page 60.

Speak

10 Ask and answer about life in the future.

- have houses under the sea?
- have robots as pets?
- cycle everywhere?
- live to the age of 120?
- fly around in 'spacecars'?
- go to the Moon for weekends?
- live on Mars?
- wear special clothes to stay cool?
- take pills as food?
- only go to online schools?

A: Will people live in houses under the sea one day?
B: Yes, I think they will./Maybe, but it won't happen in my lifetime./In my opinion, this won't happen.

Extra practice

For more practice, go to page 57.

8c If you take too long, I'll ...

Grammar	First conditional with *if*
Vocabulary	Computer language
Function	Describe and deal with computer problems

Dialogue

1 🎧 **8 06 Listen and read. Complete the dialogue with the correct phrases.**

Kiran: So this is the Tower of London.

Jodie: Yes. It's pretty amazing. It's 800 years old.

Kiran: Yes, incredible. Can we stop here a minute? I want to read about it on my tablet.

Jodie: OK, but if you take too long, I'll go in without you.

Kiran: ¹___ I can't connect to the internet.

Jodie: There's a wi-fi sign near the ticket office.

Kiran: Will I get a connection if I stand next to it?

Jodie: ²___

Kiran: OK. I'll try again.

Jodie: ³___

Kiran: No. There's something wrong.

Jodie: Maybe your battery's flat.

Kiran: No. I charged it last night.

Jodie: Maybe you need a password.

Kiran: I don't think so.

Jodie: ⁴___ Let's go and look at the Tower. It shuts at half past five.

Kiran: But I won't enjoy the visit if I don't read about it first.

Jodie: Fine! I'll go and see the Tower. You stay here and wait for a connection!

Phrases
- Just forget about it. • How annoying!
- Let's hope so. • Any luck?

Comprehension

2 **Match the beginnings (1–6) to the endings (a–f).**

1 – b

1 The Tower of London is
2 Kiran wants to read about it
3 Jodie doesn't want to
4 There's a wi-fi sign near the
5 Kiran charged his tablet
6 The Tower shuts at

a) online.
b) 800 years old.
c) half past five.
d) last night.
e) ticket office.
f) wait.

Vocabulary: Computer language

3 🎧 **8 07** **Listen and repeat. Match the numbers in the photos (1–8) to eight nouns from the box.**

1 – screen

Verbs
- attach • burn • charge • connect (to) • crash
- delete • download • open • print • receive
- save • search (for) • send • surf

Nouns
- attachment • broadband • charger
- connection • email • file • internet (net)
- keyboard • laptop • memory stick • mouse
- password • PC (desktop computer) • printer
- scanner • screen • software • tablet • virus
- website

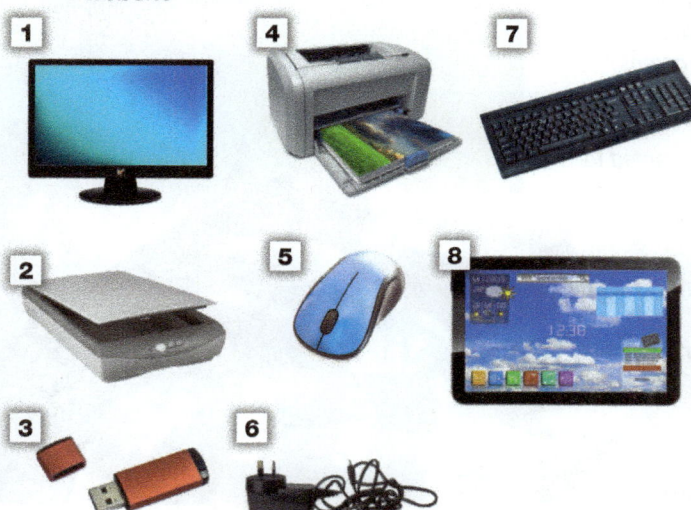

4 **What can you do on a computer? Use verbs and nouns from the box.**

send an email, surf the internet, …

Grammar

First conditional with *if*
Statements
If you **take** too long, **I'll go** without you.
If you **stand** there, you**'ll get** a connection.
I **won't enjoy** the visit **if** I **don't read** about it first.
Questions
Will I **get** a connection **if** I **stand** next to it?
What **will happen if** I **stand** there?
Short answers
Yes, I **will**./No, I **won't**.

5 **Read the dialogue again. Notice the words in red.**

Practice

6 **Write sentences using the first conditional.**

1. you (send) me those photos, I (print) them
   If you send me those photos, I'll print them.
2. there (be) a virus in that attachment, your computer (crash)
3. you (lose) my memory stick, I (be) annoyed!
4. you (delete) those big files, you (have) more space on your memory stick
5. you (not charge) your tablet now, it (not work) on the trip
6. if this laptop (crash) again, I (take) it to the computer shop

Use your English: Describe and deal with computer problems

7 🎧 **8 08** **Listen and repeat. Then practise the conversation in pairs.**

A: Mum, there's something wrong with my tablet.
B: What's the matter with it?
A: I can't connect to the internet.
B: I'll give you the new wi-fi password.
A: Thanks.

State a problem
I've got a problem with my laptop.
There's something wrong with my tablet.
Ask about a problem
What's the problem?
What's the matter with it?
What's wrong with it?
Describe a problem
It doesn't work.   It's broken.
The battery's flat.   I haven't got my charger.
I can't connect to the internet.
Offer to help
Shall I have a look at it?
Shall I try to repair it for you?
I'll lend you my charger.
I'll give you the (new) wi-fi password.
Say thank you
Yes, please. That would be great.
Thanks. That's really kind of you.

8 **Practise similar conversations.**

Extra practice

For more practice, go to page 57.

8d   Addicted to computer games

SKILLS FOCUS: LISTENING AND SPEAKING

Get started

1 How much time do you spend playing computer games? Do you ever find it hard to stop?

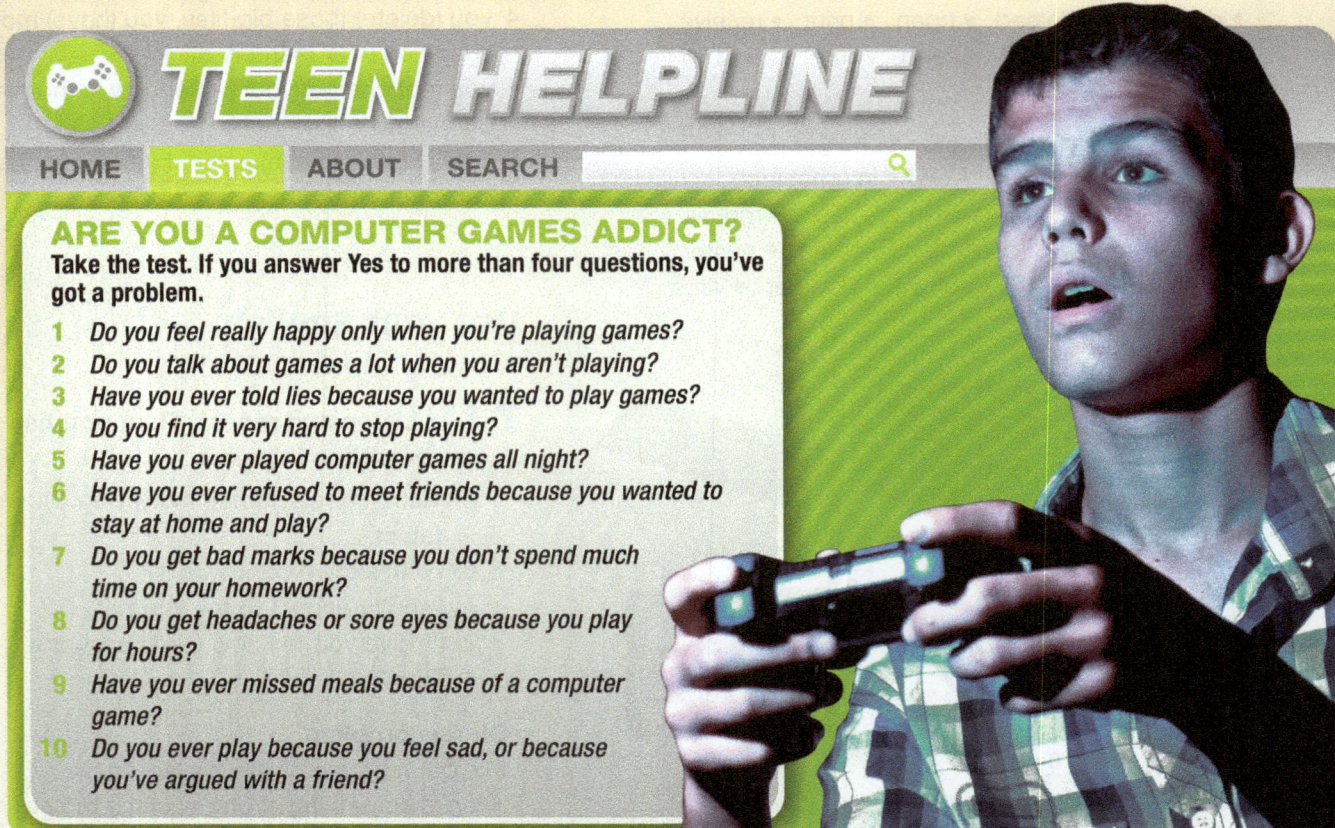

TEEN HELPLINE

HOME   TESTS   ABOUT   SEARCH

ARE YOU A COMPUTER GAMES ADDICT?
Take the test. If you answer Yes to more than four questions, you've got a problem.

1 Do you feel really happy only when you're playing games?
2 Do you talk about games a lot when you aren't playing?
3 Have you ever told lies because you wanted to play games?
4 Do you find it very hard to stop playing?
5 Have you ever played computer games all night?
6 Have you ever refused to meet friends because you wanted to stay at home and play?
7 Do you get bad marks because you don't spend much time on your homework?
8 Do you get headaches or sore eyes because you play for hours?
9 Have you ever missed meals because of a computer game?
10 Do you ever play because you feel sad, or because you've argued with a friend?

Ask Maria ✉

Hi Maria,
I took an online test and I think I'm addicted to computer games. I start playing when I get home from school. At dinner I eat fast and hurry back to my room. I tell my parents I'm going to do homework, but I just play games again. I'm doing badly at school because I do my homework in ten minutes on the bus to school. At weekends I spend ten hours a day on computer games because I just can't stop. What can I do?
Lee

Hi Lee,
Thank you for your honest email. It can be difficult to stop this addiction because we all need to use our computers every day for work, study and emails. So please tell your parents and teachers about your problem. I'm sure they can help because they'll control your time on the computer. They can also block online games on your computer. I think you'll win in the end.
Good luck!
Maria

NEW WORDS
• addict • refuse • headache • sore eyes
• argue • online • addicted • do badly
• addiction • control • block

Read

2 🎧 **8 09** **Read the test and letter from the website. How many hours does Lee spend altogether on computer games at the weekend?**

Comprehension

3 **Answer the questions.**

1 Which three questions in the test did Lee definitely answer with a 'yes'?
2 How long does he spend on his homework?
3 Where does Lee do his homework?
4 Who does Lee need to talk to about his addiction?

Speak your mind!

> **SPEAKING TIP: GIVE AND LISTEN TO OPINIONS POLITELY!**
> Useful phrases: *I think, I'm sure, In my opinion*
> While you are listening, smile, nod your head and make encouraging comments: *Right, Yes, Sure, I see, Really?*
> Now do Exercise 4.

4a **Tick (✓) the three best solutions to computer games addiction.**

1 ☐ Lee can ask his parents before he uses the computer.
2 ☐ Lee can stop using his computer for a few months.
3 ☐ Lee's parents can delete his games.
4 ☐ Lee's parents can block online games on his computer.
5 ☐ Lee can sell his computer.
6 ☐ Lee can keep his computer in the kitchen or living room.

b **In pairs, take turns giving your opinion about solutions to games addiction. Give reasons if possible.**

A: I think it's best for Lee to sell his computer. Then he can't play games.

B: Really? I think he needs his computer for homework. So in my opinion, his parents can delete his games.

Listen

> **LISTENING TIP: LISTEN MORE THAN ONCE**
> The first time you listen, don't worry about the details. Try to get the general meaning. The next time you listen you can note the details.
> Now do Exercise 5.

5a 🎧 **8 10** **Listen and tick (✓) the things Lee and his friend Phil talk about on the phone.**

☐ clothes
✓ computers
☐ friends
☐ games
☐ health
☐ holidays
☐ music
☐ school work
☐ sport

b 🎧 **8 10** **Listen again and answer the questions.**

1 What problems did Lee get from the computer?
headaches and sore eyes
2 Which game was he addicted to?
3 How many hours a week did he play?
4 When did he move to Lewes?
5 Where is his computer now?
6 What does he use it for?
7 How often does he play football?

> **SOLVE IT!**
> **6** **How long did Lee play computer games on weekdays? Use your answers to Exercise 2 and Exercise 5b, number 3 to help you.**

Write

7 **Imagine you are Lee. Write to Maria. Tell her about how you stopped your games addiction and how you spend your time now.**

Dear Maria,
Thank you for your help. I'm not addicted to computer games now. I told my mum about the problem and she ... .

Grammar (16 marks)

1 Complete what the people say about their jobs. Use *if* with the zero conditional.

0 Model: not like a dress/I/not/wear it
If I don't like a dress, I don't wear it.
1 Ski instructor: there/not be any snow/I/not work
2 Waitress: customers/be rude/it/not be easy
3 Director: people/like my films/I/feel great
4 Taxi driver: there/be bad traffic/I/not like driving
.../4

2 Complete the sentences with *'ll* or *won't*.

0 A: Do you like the red one?
B: No, I don't. I think I*'ll buy* the blue one.
1 A: I haven't got my phone.
B: Don't worry, you ___ need it.
2 A: Have you got her a present yet?
B: No, I haven't. I ___ get her one tomorrow.
3 A: You're late for class!
B: Sorry, Miss Rollins. It ___ happen again.
4 A: Where's the best place to meet?
B: I ___ come to your house.
.../4

3 Complete with the correct form of the verbs.

0 If the school library *is* shut, I*'ll do* my project at home. (be/do)
1 I ___ her some flowers if they ___ too expensive. (buy/not be)
2 If we ___ now, we ___ late. (leave/not be)
3 ___ you ___ me that photo if I ___ you my email address? (send/give)
4 They ___ us if we ___ quietly. (not hear/speak)
.../8

Vocabulary (16 marks)

4 Complete with the correct words from the box.

- big-headed • ~~funny~~ • generous
- honest • lazy • shy • untidy

0 He makes me laugh. He's *funny*.
1 He always tells the truth. He's very ___.
2 He doesn't like meeting new people. He's ___.
3 He thinks he's very clever. He's ___.
4 Her room is always in a mess. She's ___.
5 He spends all his money on friends. He's ___.
6 She never does any work. She's ___.
.../6

5 Write the weather in each city.

0 Rome
It's sunny in Rome./The sun's shining in Rome.

1 Madrid 2 Warsaw 3 London 4 Lisbon
.../4

6 Complete with a computer word.

0 I send and *receive* over 100 emails a day.
1 I'll d___d the songs to my MP3 player.
2 Why don't you a___h the file to an email?
3 To find information, I s___f the internet.
4 Oh no! I don't want my computer to c___h!
5 I need to c___t to the internet.
6 Can you p___t that map for me?
.../6

Phrases/Use your English (8 marks)

7 Complete with phrases from the box.

- How annoying! • Just forget about it.
- Let's hope so. • Any luck?

1 A: Oh no! It's raining again. B: ___
2 A: I think it'll be sunny tomorrow. B: ___
3 A: I'm trying to call her again now. B: ___
4 A: I still can't find your DVD. B: ___
.../4

8 Complete with one word in each gap.

A: I've got a ¹___ with my tablet.
B: What's ²___ with it?
A: It doesn't ³___.
B: Shall I have a ⁴___ at it?
A: Yes, please. That would be great.
.../4

LISTEN AND CHECK YOUR SCORE	
Grammar	.../16
Vocabulary	.../16
Phrases/Use your English	.../8
Total	**.../40**

Skills Revision

Read

1 **Match each person (1–5) to a holiday (A–G). There are two extra holidays.**

1 Fifteen-year-old Susanna would like an activity holiday. She'd like to do painting or dancing in a seaside place. ☐

2 Jessica wants a quiet holiday by the sea. She wants clean water, empty beaches and beautiful views. She doesn't want to go to classes. ☐

3 I'd like to visit a European city – perhaps Prague or Berlin. I like museums, art galleries, castles and concerts. *Marlene* ☐

4 I'd like a holiday in the mountains or near a lake. I enjoy walking, climbing and photography. I don't mind camping. *Stuart* ☐

5 Rory is eighteen and he wants to do sport every day. Top of his list are scuba diving, windsurfing and sailing. ☐

A Castle Tours

You'll visit a different Scottish castle every day. On your last night you'll stay in a castle in the mountains. Don't come on this holiday if you're scared of ghosts!

B Explore Europe

We have trips to all the European capitals. If you like art, music and history, this is the holiday for you!

C Highland Tours

Spend four days walking and climbing in the mountains. You'll stay in tents near a lake and you'll go home with great photos.

D Islandescapes.com

We have quiet campsites near empty beaches on beautiful islands in the UK. This holiday is not for teens who like noisy discos!

E Mediterranean Adventures

Do you like surfing, windsurfing, sailing, jet-skiing and scuba diving? We offer watersports at all our holiday centres.

F Miami Magic

You'll love staying in our hotel on the beach and going to clubs and parties every night.

G Seaview Club

We have activity holidays for under-16s in our centres near the sea. Choose from tennis, sailing, photography, art, dance and drama.

Listen

2 🔊 8 12 **Listen and tick (✓) the things Erica and Angus talk about.**

concerts ☐   language ☐   the weather ☐
food ☐   paintings ✓   transport ☐
ghosts ☐   the sea ☐

3 **Listen again and choose the correct options.**

0 Yesterday Erica
   a) went for a swim in a river.
   b) took a picture of a river.
   c) went for a walk by a river.

1 At the moment Erica is
   a) on the north coast of Scotland.
   b) on the west coast of Scotland.
   c) on the east coast of Scotland.

2 The time is
   a) 10 a.m.   b) 10 p.m.   c) 10.30 p.m.

3 The view from the window is of
   a) Lock Fine.   b) Loch Fine.   c) Loch Fyne.

4 In Scotland Erica has
   a) climbed a mountain.
   b) seen a ghost.
   c) sung Scottish songs.

Write

4 **Write an email inviting a friend to come on a trip with you next weekend. Write 80–100 words. Use the prompts to help you.**

- Say when you would like him/her to come.
- Say where you are going.
- Say how you are travelling.
- Say what you can do there.

Hi ...,
Would you like to come on a trip with me and my family ...

NOW I CAN		
Read	understand short notices about holidays.	☐
Listen	identify main topics and find specific information in a short conversation.	☐
Write	write a short email invitation.	☐

Extra practice

Unit 5

Lesson 5a

1 There was a robbery at a Brighton bank yesterday. A police officer asked two people what they were doing yesterday morning. Look at the information and complete the questions and answers.

	Alan Rigg
9.00–10.00	watch television
10.00–11.00	drive to Brighton
11.00–12.30	drink coffee with Sue Baker
	Sue Baker
9.00–10.00	read my emails at home
10.00–11.00	do some shopping in town centre
11.00–12.30	drink coffee with Alan Rigg

PC Jones: What ¹*were you doing* (you/do) yesterday morning, Mr Rigg?
Alan Rigg: Between 9 and 10. I ²___.
PC Jones: ³___ (you/still watch) TV between 10 and 11.30?
Alan Rigg: ⁴___.
PC Jones: What ⁵___ (you/do) between 11.30 and 12.30?
Alan Rigg: I ⁶___.
PC Jones: What ⁷___ (she/wear)?
Alan Rigg: She ⁸___ (wear) a green shirt and jeans.
PC Jones: Thank you. Now, Ms Baker. What were you doing between 9 and 10 yesterday morning?
Sue Baker: I ⁹___.
PC Jones: ¹⁰___ (you/still/read) your emails between 10 and 11.00?
Sue Baker: ¹¹___. I ¹²___ in the town centre.
PC Jones: And between 11.00 and 12.30?
Sue Baker: I ¹³___.
PC Jones: What ¹⁴___ (you/wear)?
Sue Baker: I ¹⁵___ (wear) a green shirt and jeans.
PC Jones: I see. Thank you, Ms Baker.

2 Change the adjectives in the box to adverbs and complete the sentences.

- good   • polite   • late   • slow   • angry
- careless   • loud   • hard

1 Hannah walks to school very *slowly*.
2 My brother usually listens to his music very ___.
3 On Saturdays, I'm always tired so I get up ___.
4 When I've got an exam, I always study ___.
5 Our team is great. We always play ___.
6 My sister gets bad marks when she does her homework ___.
7 My cousin works in a shop and she speaks very ___ to the customers.
8 My dad shouted ___ at me last night because my bedroom is so untidy.

Lesson 5b

1 Four people were in a bank when some robbers came in. Complete their statements with the correct form of the verb in brackets in the past simple or past continuous.

Martin: I ¹*was listening* (listen) to my MP3 player when the robbers ²___ (come) into the bank. While they ³___ (take) the money, I ⁴___ (get) very quietly under a desk.

Olivia: I ⁵___ (talk) to the bank manager when the robbers ⁶___ (come) in. They ⁷___ (wear) black clothes. I ⁸___ (stay) behind my desk.

Pete: I was outside the bank. I ⁹___ (wait) for my friend when the robbers ¹⁰___ (arrive). I ¹¹___ (go) across the road and ¹²___ (call) the police.

Jen: I ¹³___ (take) out some money from the cash machine when I ¹⁴___ (see) the robbers. I ¹⁵___ (run) out of the bank and into the street.

Lesson 5c

1 Write about the films using the prompts and *who, which* or *where.*

Agent Cody Banks

1 Cody Banks is a teenager/love skateboarding and hanging out with friends.
Cody Banks is a teenager who loves skateboarding and hanging out with friends.

2 But Cody has a secret/make him different from his friends.

3 He's a young CIA agent/have/a lot of adventures.

The Prince and Me

1 Paige is a young student/study medicine at university.

2 She meets a young man/be a prince called Eddie.

3 They want to get married, but can Paige live in a country/she/not know anyone?

The Lord of the Rings

1 Frodo Baggins finds a ring/have/terrible magic power.

2 Frodo takes the ring to Mordor/he must destroy it in a fire.

3 Frodo meets many strange people/help him on his journey.

2 What are the types of film in Exercise 1?

1 Agent Cody Banks ___

2 The Prince and Me ___

3 The Lord of the Rings ___

Unit 6

Lesson 6a

1 Combine the sentences with *too* or *enough.*

1 Inveraray isn't very big. It doesn't have a theatre.
Inveraray isn't big enough to have a theatre.

2 It's very dangerous. You can't skateboard here.

3 My grandparents don't live very close. They can't visit us every week.

4 Rowan is tall. She can get the apples from that tree.

5 Your car is quite big. You can't park in that space.

6 I'm really tired. I can't do my homework tonight.

7 He's rich. He can buy everything he wants.

8 It's very hot. We can't go for a run.

Lesson 6b

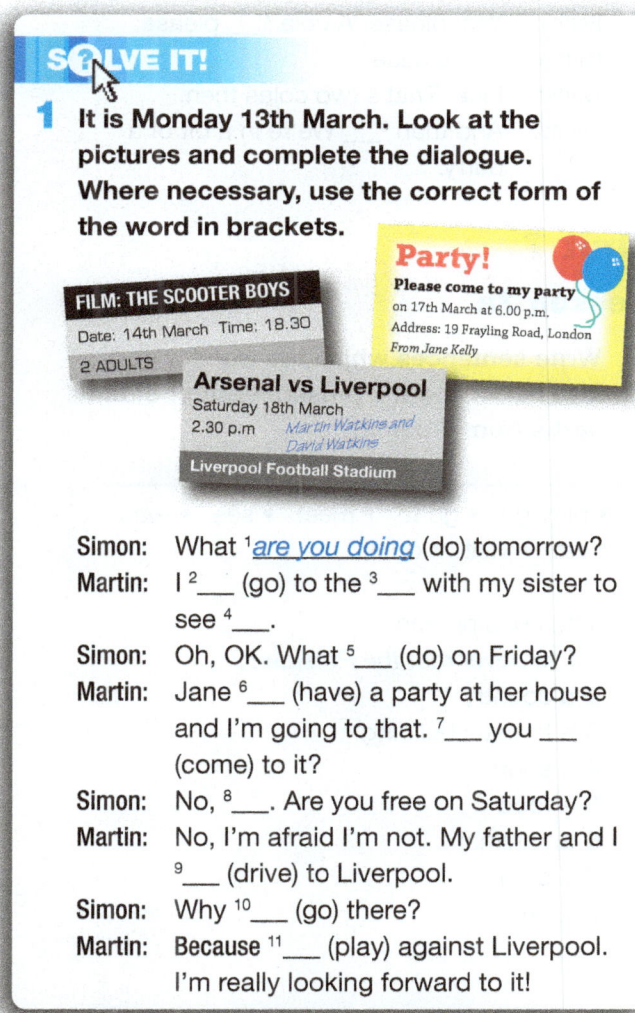

SOLVE IT!

1 It is Monday 13th March. Look at the pictures and complete the dialogue. Where necessary, use the correct form of the word in brackets.

FILM: THE SCOOTER BOYS
Date: 14th March Time: 18.30
2 ADULTS

Party!
Please come to my party
on 17th March at 6.00 p.m.
Address: 19 Frayling Road, London
From Jane Kelly

Arsenal vs Liverpool
Saturday 18th March
2.30 p.m *Martin Watkins and David Watkins*
Liverpool Football Stadium

Simon: What ¹*are you doing* (do) tomorrow?

Martin: I ²___ (go) to the ³___ with my sister to see ⁴___.

Simon: Oh, OK. What ⁵___ (do) on Friday?

Martin: Jane ⁶___ (have) a party at her house and I'm going to that. ⁷___ you ___ (come) to it?

Simon: No, ⁸___. Are you free on Saturday?

Martin: No, I'm afraid I'm not. My father and I ⁹___ (drive) to Liverpool.

Simon: Why ¹⁰___ (go) there?

Martin: Because ¹¹___ (play) against Liverpool. I'm really looking forward to it!

Lesson 6c

1 Complete the conversation with the words and phrases from the box.

- I'd   • 'll have   • ~~What would you like~~
- for me,   • Would you like   • can I
- can we have the bill, please?
- Anything else?   • Me too,

Waiter: [1]*What would you like*?
Penny: [2]___ like spaghetti bolognese, please.
Laurie: And [3]___ have baked salmon, please?
Waiter: So that's one spaghetti and one baked salmon. [4]___
Penny: Yes, I [5]___ a tomato salad too, please.
Waiter: [6]___ any drinks?
Penny: Yes, please. A cola [7]___ please.
Laurie: [8]___ please.
Waiter: Fine. That's two colas then.
Penny: And then [9]___ We're in a bit of a hurry.

Unit 7

Lesson 7a

1 Write sentences which are true for you. Use *never* and the present perfect of the verbs from the box.

- play/go   • go to   • ~~meet~~   • see   • read
- eat   • visit   • drink

1 famous person
   I've never met the President.
2 a country
3 a famous building
4 a sport
5 a food
6 an animal
7 a book
8 a drink

Lesson 7b

1 Robbie is going on holiday with his family. Look at his list and make sentences using *already* or *yet*.

1 Robbie has already packed his rucksack.

THINGS TO DO FOR MY HOLIDAY IN FLORIDA!!!!

1 pack my rucksack ✓
2 find my passport ✗
3 buy some new sunglasses ✓
4 wash my blue shorts ✓
5 text Rory ✗
6 finish my Geography project ✗

Lesson 7c

1 Write sentences using the words in brackets.

1 He's just gone out. (go out two minutes ago)
   He went out two minutes ago.
2 Carla is still doing her homework. (not/finish yet)
3 I read that book two years ago. (already/read)
4 Harry doesn't know New York. (never/go)
5 I've already been to Canada. (go/last year)
6 I bought this guitar a few days ago. (just/buy)

SOLVE IT!

2 Read the clues. Which one type of music does each person like?

1 Leo loves classical music.
2 Jessica has never liked rock music.
3 Neither Stephen nor Leo has ever bought any rap music.
4 Ellie has just bought an R & B CD for Jessica.
5 The person who likes rock is a boy.
6 Ellie is an Eminem fan.

	Rock	Classical	Rap	R & B
Leo		✓		
Jessica				
Stephen				
Ellie				

Unit 8

Lesson 8a

1 **Read the clues and complete the crossword with personality adjectives.**

Down

1 the opposite of noisy
2 the opposite of mean
4 the opposite of stupid
5 makes you laugh
8 a ___ person is a bit scared of meeting new people

Across

3 never tells lies
6 the opposite of rude
7 tells you what to do
9 the opposite of generous
10 doesn't work hard

Lesson 8b

1 **Complete the conversations about the future with the correct form of will.**

1 A: How ¹*will we get* (we/get) electricity?
   B: I think we ²___ (use) energy from the sun.
2 A: ³___ (people/buy) things in shops?
   B: No, they ⁴___. They ⁵___ (do) all their shopping online.
3 A: What ⁶___ (happen) in the kitchen?
   B: Who knows? Maybe we ⁷___ (speak) to our cooker and it ⁸___ (make) us a pizza!
4 A: And what about school? ⁹___ (there/be) teachers?
   B: Yes, there ¹⁰___. But they ¹¹___ (not/come) to school every day. Students ¹²___ (study) online a lot.
5 A: How ¹³___ (people/travel) to other countries?
   B: They ¹⁴___ (not fly). They ¹⁵___ (go) by train or boat.

Lesson 8c

1 **Complete the words with the missing vowels.**

1 scnnr
   scanner
2 mmry stck
3 dwnld
4 vrs
5 ttchmnt
6 brdbnd
7 dsktp cmptr
8 sftwr
9 kybrd
10 lptp
11 tblt

2 **Make sentences about Darren with the first conditional. The end of one sentence is the beginning of the next sentence.**

If he loses his memory stick ...

1 he/lose all his important files
   If he loses his memory stick, he'll lose all his important files.
2 he/lose his school project
   If he loses all his important files, he'll lose his school project.
3 he/be in trouble with his teacher
4 his mum/not buy him a new pair of trainers
5 he/not look cool
6 Nadia/not go to the school disco with him
7 Darren/be upset and stay at home

Unit 9

Lesson 9a

SOLVE IT!

1 Look at the pictures. Read the clues and write the names of the boys.

1 *Jerry*

2 ___

3 ___

4 ___

5 ___

- The weather's hot and sunny and Paul's clothes are right for the beach!
- Rob is smart. He's going for a job interview.
- Mark's clothes are very casual and he hates wearing plain clothes.
- Jerry is wearing clothes for cold weather.
- Tom is wearing only one colour.

Lesson 9b

1 Write conversations for each person. Use the prompts.

 **1** Tania

 **2** Anil

 **3** Cole

 **4** Ruby

 **5** Bob

 **6** Nina

You: What's the matter?
Tania: I've got toothache.
You: Poor you! You shouldn't eat any more sweet things. You should go to the dentist.

1 eat any more sweet things ✗ /go to the dentist ✓
2 be at school ✗ /stay at home ✓
3 go to the doctor ✓ /wait for it to get better ✗
4 lie down ✓ /eat anything ✗
5 read any books ✗ /take a painkiller ✓
6 take some medicine ✓ /eat any crisps ✗

Lesson 9c

1 Complete the article about David Beckham with the correct form of *(not) have to* and the verbs from the box.

- put • ~~be~~ • never/wear • go together
- not/wash • take

THE PERFECT —— MAN

David Beckham has a few problems, it seems. For David, everything [1]*has to be* clean, tidy and perfect. When he goes into a hotel room, he changes everything. 'I [2]___ everything in a straight line or in pairs.' 'When he puts his cola cans in the fridge, if there's an odd number (e.g. 1, 3 or 5), he [3]___ one away and put it in a cupboard,' says his wife, Victoria. He buys twenty pairs of socks every week, so he [4]___ his socks and he [5]___ the same pair twice. What about his shirts and sweaters? Are they all the same colour? 'No, not really,' says David, 'but all the same colours [6]___ in my wardrobe!'

Word bank

Unit 5

Lesson 5b

Prepositions of place
- behind • between • in • in front of
- near • next to • on • on the corner of
- opposite • under

Unit 6

Lesson 6a

Places in town
- bank • bookshop • bus stop • café
- car park • cashpoint • computer shop
- music shop • newsagent • park
- pharmacy • post office • restaurant
- sports centre • station • supermarket

Lesson 6b

Transport
- bike • boat • bus • car • coach • lorry
- motorbike • plane • scooter • taxi • train
- tram • underground (Tube)

Unit 7

Lesson 7a

Holiday activities
- go climbing/climb • go mountain biking
- go shopping/shop • go sightseeing/sightsee
- go skiing/ski • go snowboarding
- go sunbathing/sunbathe
- go swimming/swim • go to a museum
- go to the beach • go windsurfing/windsurf
- play beach volleyball

Lesson 7c

Types of music
- classical • country and western • folk
- heavy metal • hip-hop • jazz • Latin
- pop • R & B • rap • reggae • rock
- soul • techno

Unit 8

Lesson 8b

The weather
- cloudy • cold • foggy • freezing
- hot • raining (It's raining.)
- shining (The sun's shining.)
- snowing (It's snowing.) • sunny • warm
- windy

Unit 9

Lesson 9a

Clothes
- boots • dress • gloves • hat • jacket
- jeans • leggings • shirt • shoes • shorts
- skirt • socks • trainers • trousers • T-shirt

Pronunciation

Unit 5 Lesson 5a

🎧 5/02 **Exercise 6** /ɒ/ r<u>o</u>ck /ɔː/ s<u>a</u>w

a **Listen and repeat.**

rock	not	what	want	on
saw	always	talk	walk	morning

b **Listen and underline the /ɒ/ sounds and put a circle around the /ɔː/ sounds.**

1 I saw a rock star on the bus this morning.
2 Sonia and Don walked and talked all day.
3 What did Paul want?

Unit 6 Lesson 6c

🎧 6/07 **Exercise 4** /tʃ/ <u>ch</u>icken, /ʃ/ fi<u>sh</u>

a **Listen and repeat.**

chicken	cheese	chips	chocolate
sugar	fish	fresh	mashed potato

b **Listen and underline the /tʃ/ sounds and put a circle around the /ʃ/ sounds.**

1 Chicken and chips, please. And mashed potato.
2 Fish and chips, please. Is the fish fresh?

Unit 7 Lesson 7b

🎧 7/03 **Exercise 6** /ʊ/ b<u>oo</u>k, /uː/ y<u>ou</u>

a **Listen and repeat.**

book	look	cook	put	good
you	too	do	food	soup

b **Listen and underline the /ʊ/ sounds and put a circle around the /uː/ sounds.**

1 I bought a new cook book yesterday. Look!
2 Good. Do you want to make soup, too?
3 Can you put the food on the table?

Unit 8 Lesson 8b

🎧 8/05 **Exercise 9** /aʊ/ n<u>ow</u>, /əʊ/ sn<u>ow</u>

a **Listen and repeat.**

now	out	how	about	brown
snow	go	phone	don't	won't

b **Listen and underline the /aʊ/ sounds and put a circle around the /əʊ/ sounds.**

1 How about a pizza in town before we go home?
2 Don't phone Howard now. He won't be home till two.
3 There's no snow at Roland's house now.

Unit 9 Lesson 9a

🎧 9/03 **Exercise 6** /tʃ/ <u>ch</u>ecked, /dʒ/ <u>j</u>acket

a **Listen and repeat.**

checked	cheese	watch	which	lunch
jacket	jeans	Japanese	juice	just

b **Listen and underline the /tʃ/ sounds and put a circle around the /dʒ/ sounds.**

1 I like the checked jacket and blue jeans best.
2 Which jeans do you prefer?
3 Jake's got a Japanese watch.
4 A cheese sandwich and orange juice, please.

Word list

Unit 5

Lesson 5a
Adverbs
angrily
badly
carefully
carelessly
clearly
early
easily
fast
hard
late
loudly
noisily
politely
quickly
quietly
slowly
well

embarrassing
Have a look.
Honestly!
I expect
You're winding me up!

Lesson 5b
Prepositions of place and motion
across
along
down
into
out of
over
past
through
up

fortunately
mouse
Ouch!
pick up
plasters
scream

Lesson 5c
Types of film
action film
animated film
comedy
crime film
fantasy film
horror film
musical
romance
science fiction film
spy film
thriller
western

alien
fall in love
king
lion
magic
monkey
performance
scary
steal
tablet

Lesson 5d
alive
berry/berries
catch
give thanks
grow
harvest
low
medicine
Native American
passengers
port
religion
sailor
seasick
storm
tribe
turkey

Lesson 5e
ring (n)

Unit 6

Lesson 6a
Places in town
art gallery
hospital
hotel
library
market
museum
petrol station
police station
shopping centre
theatre
travel agent
tourist information
  centre
town hall
zoo

a long way
close (adj)
crowded
cycle path
day trip
everything
live music
royal family
safe
sunbathe
surf
village
wonderful

Lesson 6b
Transport
caravan
ferry
helicopter
minibus
moped
ship
van

holiday camp
go rollerblading
I don't believe it!
It's complicated.
miles away
Remind me.
with a bit of luck

Lesson 6c
Restaurant food
apple pie and cream
baked potatoes
baked salmon
cheesecake
chicken curry
chips
chocolate ice cream
cola
fish soup
fresh vegetables
fruit juice
fruit salad
garlic bread
garlic prawns
green salad
grilled sardines
lamb kebab
lasagne
lemonade
mashed potato
mineral water
ravioli
rice
roast chicken
spaghetti bolognese
steak
tomato salad
vanilla ice cream

bill (n)
cover charge
dessert
desserts
of course
order (v)
side order
What's the matter with
  you?
without

Lesson 6d
change (n)
charity
dishonest
envelope
fault
get into trouble
honest
money
notice
owner
poor
save
tip

Unit 7

Lesson 7a
bear
desert
dog sledding
jealous
ocean
pack (v)
ride a snowmobile

Lesson 7b
accident
calm down
How disgusting!
How horrible!
lottery
online
That's a pity!
That's a shame.
That's awful!
That's incredible!
The trouble is
What a nightmare!
What a pity!
What a surprise!
What do you reckon?
You mean

Lesson 7c
audition
fan
hit (n)
judge
loser
opera
record
talent show
winner

Lesson 7d
alligator
dolphin
excellent
fabulous
fishing village
giant
go snorkelling
go scuba diving
mangrove
multi-coloured
painting
seal
skyscraper
stormy
without

Unit 8

Lesson 8a

Personality adjectives
annoying
bad-tempered
big-headed
bossy
clever
cute
easy-going
friendly
funny
generous
hard-working
helpful
honest
kind
lazy
loyal
mean
polite
quiet
rude
shy
tidy
unfriendly
untidy

wolf/wolves
lamb
seat (n)
look out of
stand up
turn on
half
marks
shut
exactly

Lesson 8b
bicycle
cool
Earth
electric
energy
everywhere
future
Mars
pill
robot
sick
temperature
work (n)

Lesson 8c
Computer language
attach
attachment
broadband
burn
charge
charger
connect to
connection
crash
delete
download
email
file
internet (net)
keyboard
laptop
memory stick
mouse
open
password
PC (desktop computer)
print
printer
receive
save
scanner
screen
search (for)
send
software
surf
tablet
virus
website

Any luck?
broken
Fine!
flat (adj)
have a look
How annoying!
Just forget about it.
Let's hope so.
repair (v)
sign
something wrong
visit (n)
What's wrong?
wi-fi

Lesson 8d
addict
addicted
addiction
argue
block
control
do badly
headache
in my opinion
online
refuse
sore eyes

Unit 9

Lesson 9a

Clothes, accessories and styles

baggy
baseball cap
belt
casual
checked
flowery
patterned
plain
pocket
scarf
sleeveless
smart
spotted
striped
tie
tight
zip

bow tie
In that case,
It cost a fortune
It's more my style.
It suits you.
Rubbish!
school prom
size

Lesson 9b

Illness

a cold
a cough
a headache
a sore throat
a temperature
earache
stomachache
toothache
flu
I don't feel very well.
I feel ill/sick/hot.
My (ankle) hurts.

cough mixture
painkiller
throat pastilles
turn off

Lesson 9c

Household jobs

do the cleaning
do the cooking
do the ironing
do the shopping
do the washing
do the washing-up
do the vacuuming
empty the dishwasher
lay the table
make breakfast/lunch/
  dinner
make the bed
take the rubbish out
tidy your room
wash the car

awesome
cabin
canoeing
maple syrup
summer camp
waffles

Lesson 9d

birthplace
carnival
costume
create (v)
crown
dress up (v)
found (v)
gospel
grow/grew (v)
instrument
jewellery
mask
necklace
nickname
parade
population

Lesson 9e

high heels
thin

Irregular verbs

Infinitive	Past	Past participle
be	was/were	been
become	became	become
begin	began	begun
break	broke	broken
bring	brought	brought
burn	burnt	burnt
buy	bought	bought
catch	caught	caught
choose	chose	chosen
come	came	come
cost	cost	cost
do	did	done
dream	dreamt	dreamt
drink	drank	drunk
drive	drove	driven
eat	ate	eaten
fall	fell	fallen
feel	felt	felt
find	found	found
fly	flew	flown
forget	forgot	forgotten
get	got	got
give	gave	given
go	went	gone/been
have	had	had
hear	heard	heard
hit	hit	hit
hurt	hurt	hurt
keep	kept	kept
know	knew	known
learn	learnt	learnt
leave	left	left
lose	lost	lost

Infinitive	Past	Past participle
make	made	made
meet	met	met
pay	paid	paid
put	put	put
read	read	read
ride	rode	ridden
ring	rang	rung
run	ran	run
say	said	said
see	saw	seen
sell	sold	sold
send	sent	sent
shine	shone	shone
sing	sang	sung
sit	sat	sat
sleep	slept	slept
speak	spoke	spoken
spend	spent	spent
stand	stood	stood
sting	stung	stung
swim	swam	swum
take	took	taken
teach	taught	taught
tear	tore	torn
tell	told	told
think	thought	thought
throw	threw	thrown
understand	understood	understood
wake	woke	woken
wear	wore	worn
win	won	won
write	wrote	written

9a   Which ones are best?

Grammar   *Which* + indefinite pronoun *one/ones*
Vocabulary Clothes, accessories and styles
Function   Choosing clothes to wear

Vocabulary: Clothes, accessories and styles

1a **Recall** Write all the clothes you can remember. Then check the Word bank on page 59.

b 🎧 **Extension** Listen and repeat. Look at the clothes (1–8) and describe them. Use the words in the box.

1 A red and black spotted hat.
2 A striped scarf.

Accessories
- baseball cap   • belt   • pocket
- scarf   • tie   • zip

Style
- baggy   • casual   • sleeveless   • smart
- tight

Pattern
- checked   • flowery   • patterned   • plain
- spotted   • striped

Dialogue

2 🎧 **Listen and read. Complete the dialogue with the correct phrases.**

Tom and Emma are getting ready for the school dance.

Tom: Wow! Is that a new skirt?
Emma: Yes, ¹___ but now Mum says it's too tight.
Tom: ²___ You look fantastic.
Emma: Thank you. Where's your bow tie?
Tom: I hate ties.
Emma: But you can't go to the dance without one. Have you got one?
Tom: Yes, two, actually. Which one do you like?
Emma: The checked one.
Tom: Well, I prefer the plain one.
        ³___
Emma: ⁴___ can I wear the other one?
Tom: Er ... are you sure? You aren't wearing a shirt.
Emma: I know, but I can put it in my hair. Like this. What do you reckon?
Tom: Nice. It suits you.
Emma: Now shoes. Which ones are best?
Tom: These ones maybe?
Emma: Ha ha, very funny!

Phrases
- In that case,   • It's more my style.
- it cost a fortune,   • Rubbish!

Comprehension

3 **Answer true (T), false (F) or doesn't say (DS).**

1 Emma is wearing a new skirt. *T*
2 Emma's mum doesn't like the colour of her skirt.
3 The school dance is tonight.
4 Tom doesn't like the bow tie in Emma's hair.
5 Emma hasn't got any shoes.

Grammar

Which + indefinite pronoun one/ones
Singular
Which one do you like?
This/That/The checked **one**.
Plural
Which ones are best?
These/Those/The black **ones**.

4 Read the dialogue again. Notice the words in red.

Practice

5 Complete the dialogues with *one* or *ones*.

1 A: Which trainers do you like?
  B: I like the blue and white *ones*

2 A: Where's my shirt?
  B: Which ___ do you want?
  A: The plain yellow ___.

3 Which jeans do you like best? The tight ___ or the baggy ___?

4 A: Where's my jacket?
  B: Which ___? You've got lots of jackets.

5 A: Can I wear your gloves please? It's freezing outside.
  B: Yes, you can have my red ___.

Pronunciation: /tʃ/ checked, /dʒ/ jacket

6 🎧 9 03 Go to page 60.

Use your English: Choosing clothes to wear

7 🎧 9 04 Listen and repeat. Then practise the conversation in pairs.

A: Do you like this <u>new checked shirt</u>?
B: Yes. It suits you.
A: Which <u>jeans</u> shall I wear with it?
B: Why don't you wear your <u>black ones</u>?
A: Hmm… I prefer <u>these blue ones</u>. How do I look?
B: You look good. … Actually, I think the <u>jeans are a bit tight</u>.

Ask for opinions
Do you like my new (shirt/shoes)?
What do you reckon?
How does it/do they look?
Does it/Do they suit me? How do I look?
Make positive comments
(Yes.) It looks good./They look good.
(Yes.) It suits you./They suit you.
(Yes.) You look fantastic/nice.
Make negative comments
It's/They're too (baggy/tight).
It doesn't/They don't suit you.
It's/They're the wrong size.
Ask for advice
What shall I wear (with it)?
Make suggestions
Why don't you wear the/your …?
Ask about preferences
Which one/ones do you like/prefer?
State a preference
I like/prefer the green one/ones.

8 Change the underlined words in Exercise 7 and practise similar conversations.

1 new black jacket/trousers?/striped?/prefer … red/✓ fantastic

2 checked shirt/skirt?/green?/prefer … purple/✗ skirt baggy

3 new red dress/shoes?/red?/prefer … black/✓ nice

4 spotted tie/shirt?/plain white?/prefer … pink/✗ shirt tight

Extra practice

For more practice, go to page 58.

9b You should go to bed.

Grammar *Should/Shouldn't*
Vocabulary Illness

Dialogue

1 🎧 **9·05** **Listen and read. How many people phone Jodie?**

Emma: Hi, Jodie. Are you going to come to the concert tonight?

Jodie: No. I've got a sore throat and earache.

Emma: You poor thing. You **should go** to bed.

Jodie: I *am* in bed. You've just woken me up.

Emma: Sorry. Get better soon.

…

Tom: Hi, Jodie. Emma says you're ill.

Jodie: Yes. I feel terrible and my throat really hurts.

Tom: You **shouldn't go** to the concert tonight then. You **should stay** in bed and drink lots of water.

Jodie: OK. Bye.

…

Kiran: Hello, Jodie. Tom says you don't feel very well.

Jodie: No, I don't.

Kiran: You **should try** to sleep.

Jodie: But I can't with all these phone calls. What **should** I **do**?

Kiran: You **should turn** your phone off.

Jodie: OK.

Kiran: And Jodie, you **should take** a painkiller, OK? Jodie? Jodie? I don't believe it. She's turned her phone off!

Comprehension

2 **Choose the correct options.**

1 Where is Emma going to be tonight?
   a) at a concert   b) at Jodie's house
2 Where is Jodie?
   a) in bed   b) at a concert
3 How does Jodie feel?
   a) tired   b) ill
4 What is Kiran's advice?
   a) to phone him   b) to sleep
5 What does Jodie do?
   a) She turns her phone off.
   b) She takes a painkiller.

Vocabulary: Illness

3 🎧 9 06 **Listen and repeat. Then look at the pictures (1–9) and say what is wrong.**

1 I've got earache.

I've got …	• a cold • a cough • a headache
	• a sore throat • a temperature
	• earache • stomachache
	• toothache • flu
• I don't feel very well. • I feel ill/sick/hot.	
• My (ankle) hurts.	

Grammar

Should/Shouldn't	
Affirmative	**Negative**
You **should** try to sleep.	You **shouldn't go** to the concert.
Questions	**Answers**
What **should** I **do**? **Should** I **go** to the concert?	Yes, you **should**. No, you **shouldn't**.
▶ **Now make sentences with *he*, *we* and *they*.**	

4 **Read the dialogue again. Notice the words in red.**

Practice

5 **Complete the sentences with *should* or *shouldn't*.**

1 Mum's got flu. She *should* stay in bed.
2 I've got a sore throat. I think I ___ have a hot lemon and honey drink.
3 Dan's got toothache. He ___ go to the dentist.
4 Pam's got stomachache. What ___ she do?
5 I don't feel very well. Maybe I ___ go to the party.
6 A: I've got a headache.
   B: You ___ take a painkiller.
7 A: I feel ill.
   B: You ___ go to school today.
8 A: My leg really hurts.
   B: You ___ play tennis today.

Listen

6 🎧 9 07 **Listen. What advice does the doctor give Charlie?**

1 _____   3 _____
2 _____   4 _____

S?LVE IT!

7 **In which month does Charlie visit the doctor?**

Speak

8 **Talk about illnesses. Choose the best advice from the box. Use the prompts.**

A: You don't look very well. Are you OK?
B: Not really. I've got a bad headache.
A: Oh dear! You should take a painkiller.
B: That's a good idea. Thanks.

- stay at home • put some ice on it
- take some cough mixture
- see a doctor/dentist
- drink lots of water • take a painkiller
- go to bed • get some throat pastilles

Extra practice

For more practice, go to page 58.

9c We have to make our beds.

Grammar *Have to/Don't have to*

Want to, Want + object pronoun + *to*

Vocabulary Household jobs

Read

1 Listen and read Lauren's email from summer camp in the USA. How often does Lauren do sports?

Hi Beth,

I'm having a great time at camp. I'm in the Catskill Mountains in New York State and there's a big lake where we swim and go canoeing. We do sports every day AND I'm learning to ride a horse. It's awesome!

But it's not all fun. We have to get up at seven. Breakfast is at half past seven. We don't have to cook the breakfast, but we have to do the washing-up. The breakfast here is great, especially the waffles with maple syrup. After breakfast, we have to make our beds and tidy the cabin where we sleep. One person has to take the rubbish out and another person has to do the vacuuming.

Then it's time to go out and have fun!

In the evening after dinner we sit and talk. A girl called Nicole plays the guitar and we sometimes sing. I want to learn the guitar and I want her to teach me. She's brilliant.

I've met a really nice boy called Toby. He says he loves camp, but he doesn't like doing the jobs every day. At home he doesn't have to tidy his room and he doesn't have to take out the rubbish. He's SO lucky!

Bye for now,

Lauren 😃

Comprehension

2 Correct the sentences.

1 Lauren is having a boring time at camp.
   No. Lauren is having a great time at camp.

2 Lauren is learning to swim.

3 She has waffles for dinner.

4 They never sing songs after dinner.

5 Toby doesn't like camp.

Vocabulary: Household jobs

3 Listen and repeat. Match the pictures (1–8) to phrases from the box. Which phrases are not in the pictures?

1 lay the table

- do the cleaning • do the cooking
- do the ironing • do the shopping
- do the washing • do the washing-up
- do the vacuuming
- empty the dishwasher • lay the table
- make breakfast/lunch/dinner
- make the bed • take the rubbish out
- tidy your room • wash the car

Grammar

Have to/Don't have to	
Affirmative	
One person **has to** take the rubbish out.	
We **have to** make our beds.	
Negative	
He **doesn't have to** tidy his room.	
We **don't have to** cook the breakfast.	
Yes/No questions	Short answers
Do you **have to** cook breakfast?	Yes, we **do**./No, we **don't**.
Does he **have to** tidy his room?	Yes, he **does**./No, he **doesn't**.

4 Read the email again. Notice the words in red.

Practice

5 Use the prompts to write sentences and questions.

1 I/wash my dad's car
  I have to wash my dad's car.
2 my brother/not/tidy his room
3 my dad/do the ironing on Saturday
4 we/not/lay the table on Sunday
5 your brothers/make their beds?
6 you/cook/breakfast?

Grammar

Want to
I **want to** learn the guitar.
He **doesn't want to** clean the cabin.
Want + object pronoun + *to*
I **want her to** teach me the guitar.

Practice

6 Complete Beth's postcard to Lauren with the correct form of *want to* and the verb in brackets.

Hi Lauren,

Thanks for the email. Your holiday sounds great. I ¹*want to go* (go) to summer camp with you. I ² ___ (learn) to ride a horse and I ³ ___ (swim) in that lake. It looks fantastic! My parents ⁴ ___ (me/go camping) in Cornwall, with my cousins next year. I really like Cornwall, but I ⁵ ___ (not stay) there all summer. I ⁶ ___ (visit) another country. I've never been to America. My brother ⁷ ___ (come) to summer camp, too, but he ⁸ ___ (not do) any sports. He hates sports! He just ⁹ ___ (meet) American girls!

Our holiday finishes tomorrow, but I ¹⁰ ___ (not go) home! I love Scotland.

Bye for now,

Beth

Speak

7 Talk about what you want to do this weekend and what you have to do.

Want to:
• go shopping
• go skateboarding
• go to a party
• meet friends
• play tennis
• sleep
• watch a film

Have to:
• do my homework
• do the cleaning
• do the ironing
• do the vacuuming
• make lunch
• tidy my room
• wash the car

A: *I want to go shopping with my friends on Saturday morning but I can't.*
B: *Why not?*
A: *I have to do the vacuuming and tidy my room.*
B: *What about Saturday afternoon?*
A: *I have to do my homework!*

Write

8 Write a blog about this weekend. Use *want to/don't want to* and *have to/don't have to*.

BLOG

23 February 9.30 a.m.

It's Saturday morning and it's a beautiful sunny day. This morning I want to ..., but I can't because I have to ... . My mum wants me to ... It's OK because this afternoon my mum says I don't have to ...

Extra practice

For more practice, go to page 58.

9d It's a huge street party.

SKILLS FOCUS: READING

Get started

1 What is the most famous festival in your country? Which festivals would you like to go to in other countries?

Read

2 🎧 9/10 **Read and find:**

- a nickname for New Orleans (paragraph 1)
- the size of its population in 1900 (paragraph 2)
- the name of a big music festival (paragraph 3)
- the name of the Mardi Gras carnival king (paragraph 4)

1 New Orleans in Louisiana, in the south of the USA, has a famous nickname – 'the Big Easy'. But people in New Orleans don't use that name. They call it 'Nawlins'. That isn't a nickname. That's their pronunciation! New Orleans is famous for its history, its jazz and its Mardi Gras festival.

2 The French founded New Orleans in 1718, then gave the city to the Spanish in 1763. During the nineteenth century, New Orleans became an important port. The population grew from about 10,000 in 1800 to 287,000 in 1900. There were Native Americans, African, French, Spanish, Italian, German and Caribbean people.

3 People call New Orleans the birthplace of jazz because African-Americans created jazz there. The Original Dixieland Jazz Band was from New Orleans and they made the world's first jazz record in 1917. Every year there's a huge jazz festival in the city – Jazz Fest. There isn't just jazz. You can hear gospel, R & B, folk, rock and rap. You can also buy jewellery, paintings and musical instruments at the Jazz Fest markets.

4 New Orleans' biggest festival is Mardi Gras. It started around 1740. It's a huge street party with parades. Everyone dresses up and lorries carry huge statues and people in costumes and masks through the streets. The people on the lorries throw necklaces at the crowds. Every year there is a carnival king called Rex. Rex wears a crown and often has gold clothes.

NEW WORDS
- nickname • found (v) • century
- population • grow/grew (v) • birthplace
- create (v) • gospel • jewellery • instrument
- parade • dress up (v) • costume • mask
- necklace • carnival • crown

To find the main ideas of a text quickly, read the first sentence of each paragraph. It will tell you about the topic of the paragraph.

Now do Exercise 3.

3 Match each heading (a–d) to one paragraph (1–4).

a) Jazz in New Orleans   paragraph ___
b) The city's names   paragraph ___
c) New Orleans' biggest festival   paragraph ___
d) The people of New Orleans   paragraph ___

Comprehension

4 Answer the questions.

1 Which state is New Orleans in? *Louisiana*
2 When did the French give New Orleans to the Spanish?
3 When did the first jazz record come out?
4 Around which year did Mardi Gras start in New Orleans?
5 What do people throw from the lorries?

Listen

5 🎧 Listen and answer true (T) or false (F).

1 Notting Hill Carnival is in East London. *F*
2 It's a Caribbean festival.
3 It's always on the last Sunday and Monday in August.
4 It started in 1956.
5 About 100,000 people come to the carnival.
6 You can only get Caribbean food at the carnival.
7 There are dancers in costumes on lorries.
8 Most dancers wear black costumes.
9 There's a lot of different Caribbean music.

Speak

6 Imagine you are spending August in London. Persuade a friend to go with you to the Notting Hill Carnival. He/She has lots of questions.

You: *Shall we go to Notting Hill carnival?*
Your friend: *Where's Notting Hill?*

- Where/Notting Hill?
- When/the carnival?
- What sort of carnival?
- Very popular?
- What food/eat?
- What/you see and do there?
- What costumes/wear?
- What type of music/they play?

Project

7 Write about a festival in your country.

- What's the name of the festival?
- Where is it?
- When is it?
- Is there special food at this festival?
- Is there music at this festival? What type?
- Are there special costumes? What kind of clothes do people wear?

SKILLS FOCUS: WRITING AN OPINION LETTER

WRITING TIP: GIVING AN OPINION

Useful phrases for giving an opinion:
*In my opinion, I think, I don't think,
everyone knows that*
We often make generalisations using
adverbs and quantifiers:
*often, usually, sometimes
all (of), most (of), some (of), a few*

3 Read the letter again. Circle six
opinion phrases, adverbs and
quantifiers from the Writing tip box.

4 Complete the letter to a magazine
with the phrases from the box.

- usually   • Everyone knows
- In my opinion,   • Most of   • often

Get ready to write

1 Read the letter to a teen magazine. Why doesn't
Camilla like baggy trousers?

> I didn't like the fashion photos last month.
> In my opinion, all the models were too thin. I
> think you should show healthy models of all sizes
> because teenagers often copy models. Also, I
> don't think the clothes were very practical. Clothes
> should be comfortable and easy to wear. Most of
> these clothes weren't. High heels and tight skirts
> look good, but everyone knows that it's difficult
> to walk in them. And I don't like baggy trousers
> because they sometimes fall down. Embarrassing!

I think sports centres and tennis
courts should be free for teenagers.
It costs £4 for a sixteen-year-old
to use a swimming pool and £7 to
use a tennis court in the park.
¹_____ that's too expensive. ²_____
my friends like swimming and other
sports. Very ³_____ we want to
go swimming or play tennis at the
weekend and in our holidays. But
⁴_____ we don't because we
haven't got enough money. ⁵_____
that sport is good for our health.
So let's have free sports centres for
teenagers.

James

2 Complete the sentences with the adjectives from the
box.

- easy   • embarrassing   • thin   • practical
- comfortable   • difficult

1 Camilla says the people in the photos were too ___.
2 In her opinion the clothes weren't ___.
3 She likes clothes which are ___ and ___ to wear.
4 She thinks it is ___ to walk when you wear high heels.
5 She thinks baggy trousers are ___.

Write

5 Write an email to a magazine.

- Give your opinion about one of these
  ideas:
  Cinema tickets should be cheaper for
  teenagers.
  Public transport should be free for
  teenagers.
- Use phrases from the Writing tip box.
  I think ... should be ...

Language Revision

Grammar (19 marks)

1 **Complete with *the one* or *the ones* and the adjective in brackets.**

Holly: Which T-shirt do you like?
Carla: I like ⁰*the black one*. (black)
Holly: Next picture. Which boots do you like?
Carla: I think I like ¹___. (red)
Holly: And which shirt do you like?
Carla: I prefer ²___. (checked)
Holly: Now, which trousers do you like?
Carla: I'm not sure. I think I like ³___. (blue)
Holly: Which hat do you like best?
Carla: I like ⁴___. (striped)
Holly: OK. And finally, which leggings do you like?
Carla: I like ⁵___. (plain)

.../5

2 **Write one sentence with *should* and one sentence with *shouldn't*.**

0 I'm really tired today. (go to bed early/ go out tonight)
You should go to bed early. You shouldn't go out tonight.
1 She doesn't feel well. (go home/stay at school)
2 I'm very unfit. (go for a run now/eat all those chocolates)
3 My brother has a headache. (drink some water/ sit in the sun)

.../6

3 **Complete with the correct form of *have to*.**

Mark: I ⁰*have to* do a lot of jobs in the house.
Ben: What ¹___ you ___ do?
Mark: I ²___ tidy my room, do the vacuuming and do the washing-up. Luckily I ³___ do the ironing. My mum did it this morning. ⁴___ you ___ do housework every day?
Ben: Yes, I do, because my mum ⁵___ go to work. But I ⁶___ do everything. My dad does the shopping. ⁷___ your sister ___ do any housework?
Mark: Yes, she does. She's always very helpful. But my dad ⁸___ do any housework because he's working in France at the moment.

.../8

Vocabulary (13 marks)

4 **Complete the sentences.**

0 Have you got a painkiller? I've got a *headache*.
1 I've got ___. I think that food was bad.
2 I'm going home. I don't ___ well.
3 Ouch! My arm ___.
4 I got water in my ear and now I've got ___.
5 I can't eat any biscuits. I've got a sore ___.
6 With flu, you usually have a high ___.
7 I need to see the dentist. I've got ___.

.../7

5 **Complete with household jobs.**

0 I made lunch so can you do the *washing-up*?
1 Dinner's nearly ready. Can you ___ the table?
2 We need some food. Can you do the ___?
3 Please clean the kitchen and take the ___ out.
4 My jeans are dirty. I need to do the ___.
5 I want you to ___ your room. It's a mess!
6 Dad is going to give me £5 if I ___ his car.

.../6

Phrases/Use your English (8 marks)

6 **Choose the correct response.**

1 Do you like this green dress?
2 I love that hat. It's brilliant!
3 Jake thinks his jeans are too baggy.
4 I only want one bar of chocolate.

a) Thanks. It cost a fortune.
b) In that case can I have the other one?
c) Rubbish! They're great.
d) I think the blue one is more my style.

.../4

7 **Look at the jumbled conversation. Number the lines in the correct order.**

☐ a) I think it's too tight.
☐ b) Which dress do you prefer?
☐ c) No, it isn't. It suits you.
☐ d) I like the green one best.

.../4

🎧 LISTEN AND CHECK YOUR SCORE	
Grammar	.../19
Vocabulary	.../13
Phrases/Use your English	.../8
Total	**.../40**

2B
SPLIT EDITION

LIVE Beat

WORKBOOK

Rod Fricker

Pearson Education Limited
Edinburgh Gate
Harlow
Essex CM20 2JE
England
and Associated Companies throughout the world.

www.pearsonELT.com

© Pearson Education Limited 2015

The right of Rod Fricker to be identified as author of this Work has been asserted by them in accordance with the Copyright, Designs and Patents Act 1988.

First published 2015

ARP impression 98

ISBN: 978-1-292-10195-8

Set in Helvetica Neue LT Std 55 Roman 10/14pt

Printed in Great Britain by Ashford Colour Press Ltd.

Acknowledgements

The publisher would like to thank the following for their kind permission to reproduce their photographs:

(Key: b-bottom; c-centre; l-left; r-right; t-top)

Alamy Images: Angela Hampton Picture Library 80t, dbimages 84, Dennis Hallinan 94br, Andres Rodriguez 80b, Gordon Scammell 86; **Corbis:** Patrice Latron 71, Byron Purvis 88br; **Fotolia.com:** Cristovao31 97cl, Savage ultralight 103cl; **Rex Features:** Martin Karius 91, SNAP 88tl; **The Kobal Collection:** 93tl, 93tr, 93cl, 93cr, 93bl, 93br

Cover image: *Front*: **Shutterstock.com:** Ollyy

All other images © Pearson Education

Every effort has been made to trace the copyright holders and we apologise in advance for any unintentional omissions. We would be pleased to insert the appropriate acknowledgement in any subsequent edition of this publication.

Illustrated by:

David Banks; Adrian Barclay (Beehive Illustration); Kathy Baxendale; Kel Dyson (Bright Agency); Pete Ellis; Kevin Hopgood (Beehive Illustration); Richard Jones (Beehive Illustration); Joanna Kerr (New Division); Mike Lacey (Beehive Illustration); David Shenton; Eric Smith; Jane Smith; James Walmesley (Graham-Cameron Illustrations)

Contents

5a He was wearing weird clothes.

Phrases

1 ⭐ **Complete the dialogue with the phrases from the box.**

> • have a look • honestly • I expect
> • you're winding me up

Dave: Hey! [1] *Have a look* at Martin's blog. His family are moving to Australia.

Will: [2] _____.

Dave: No, [3] _____. It's here. Look. 'Three weeks to go.'

Will: Wow! You're right. Why didn't he tell us? We were talking to him earlier today. He didn't say anything.

Dave: [4] _____ he's upset. He knows we read this and it's easier to write it than talk about it.

Grammar: Past continuous

2 ⭐ **Complete the sentences with the correct form of the verbs in brackets.**

Last Saturday at 10 a.m. …

1 I (do) *was doing* my homework.

2 my mum (cook) _____ dinner.

3 my dad (work) _____ in the garden.

4 my friends (shop) _____.

5 my two brothers (play) _____ computer games.

On Sunday at the same time…

6 I (write) _____ my blog.

7 my parents (eat) _____ breakfast.

8 my friends (play) _____ tennis.

9 my brother, Jim, (swim) _____.

10 my other brother, Tim, (wait) _____ for his girlfriend.

3 ⭐⭐ **Write true sentences about what was happening at 7 p.m. Use the verbs from the box.**

> • play • sit • have (x2) • listen to • do
> • eat • read • drive • watch

1 I *wasn't doing* my homework. I *was reading* a book.

2 My mum _____ television. She _____ the radio.

3 My friends _____ tennis. They _____ pizza.

4 My brother _____ a shower. He _____ a bath.

5 My grandparents _____. They _____ on a train.

Vocabulary: Adverbs

4 ⭐ **Choose the correct options.**

I wanted to be in the school show, but I'm not very ¹ **good** / **well** at dancing or singing. I tried acting, but the teacher told me I was very ² **quiet** / **quietly**. 'Speak more ³ **loud** / **loudly**,' she said, but it was no good. I tried doing sports, but I run very ⁴ **slow** / **slowly** and I play football very ⁵ **bad** / **badly**. Finally, I went to the school newspaper. They asked me to write something. They said that my writing was very ⁶ **clear** / **clearly** and interesting. The best thing was that it was ⁷ **easy** / **easily** for me. It's great to know that I can do one thing ⁸ **good** / **well** at least!

5 ⭐⭐ **Complete the sentences with the correct form of the words in capitals.**

1 EASY

The test was _easy_. I passed it _easily_.

2 GOOD

My sister is a _____ dancer. She dances really _____.

3 LOUD

Dad was talking _____. He is always _____ when he's excited.

4 CLEAR

Please speak _____. We need an actor with a nice, _____ voice.

5 SLOW

This isn't a _____ car, but my dad drives very _____.

6 POLITE

My cousin is very _____. She always asks for things very _____.

7 NOISE

The class worked _____. They are a very _____ class.

Grammar summary

Past continuous	
Affirmative	**Negative**
I **was working**.	I **wasn't cooking**.
You **were sleeping**.	You **weren't running**.
He/She/It **was swimming**.	He/She/It **wasn't eating**.
We/They **were playing**.	We/They **weren't making** a cake.
Questions	**Short answers**
Was he **helping** you?	Yes, he **was**. No, he **wasn't**.
Were they **singing**?	Yes, they **were**. No, they **weren't**.
Wh- **questions**	
What **were** you **doing**? Where **was** he **going**?	

Note

Usage

- We use the past continuous to talk about something that was happening or was in progress at a certain time in the past. We don't know exactly when the activity started or finished.

  At seven o'clock, I was eating dinner.
  On Friday night, we were having a party.

Form

- We form the past continuous like the present continuous, but with the past form of the verb *to be*.

  He is swimming (now). He was swimming (yesterday).
  They are shopping (now). They were shopping (at nine o'clock this morning).

Common mistakes

~~What you were doing?~~ ✗
What were you doing? ✓
~~We was doing a test.~~ ✗
We were doing a test. ✓

5b I was cycling when …

1 ⭐ **Complete the sentences with the correct form of the verbs in brackets.**

1 I (walk) *was walking* home when it (start) *started* raining.
2 We (drive) _____ home when the police (stop) _____ us.
3 I (find) _____ a great website while I (surf) _____ the internet.
4 They (eat) _____ dinner when we (arrive) _____.
5 The phone (ring) _____ while we (watch) _____ television.
6 He (swim) _____ when he (see) _____ the shark.
7 Dad (get) _____ home while mum (cook) _____ dinner.
8 When I (come) _____ home from the disco, my parents (wait) _____ for me.

2 ⭐⭐ **Combine the two sentences. Start with *while* and *when*.**

1 I was reading. My friend phoned.
 While *I was reading, my friend phoned.*
 When *my friend phoned, I was reading.*
2 My friend came to my house. I was having a shower.
 While _____.
 When _____.
3 We were shopping. We met our friends.
 While _____.
 When _____.
4 Our teacher's phone started ringing. We were having a test.
 When _____.
 While _____.
5 I left for school. My brother was still sleeping.
 When _____.
 While _____.

3 ⭐⭐ **Complete the story with the phrases from the box.**

- ~~was walking~~ • jumped • was doing
- were walking • was trying
- was looking • drove • noticed
- were taking • looked • was watching

[1] I *was walking* into town last Saturday when I [2] _____ a strange man next to a car. He [3] _____ to open the car door. When I [4] _____ again, he was next to a different car. This time, the door was open and he [5] _____ inside.
While he [6] _____ this, a police car [7] _____ past and stopped. Then two police officers got out. While they [8] _____ towards the man, he [9] _____ out of the car and ran away.
Later, I [10] _____ TV when I saw the man on the news. The police [11] _____ him to the police station in their car. He wasn't very happy.

Vocabulary: Prepositions of place and motion

4 ⭐ **Label the pictures with the correct preposition.**

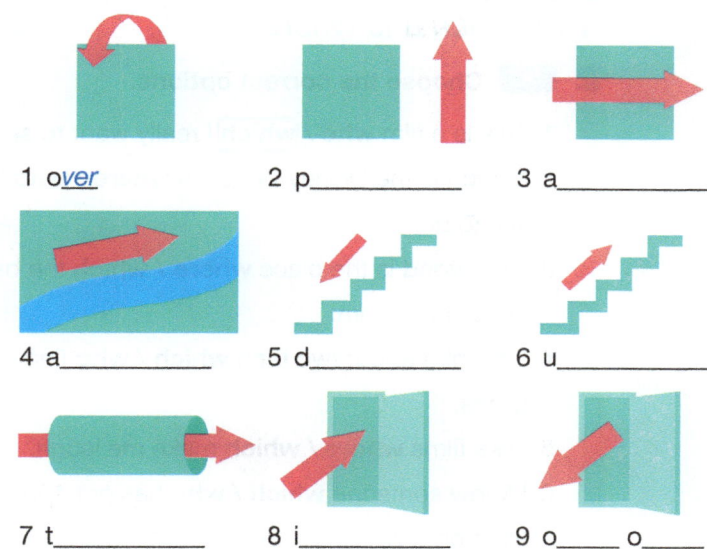

1 o*ver*   2 p_____   3 a_____

4 a_____   5 d_____   6 u_____

7 t_____   8 i_____   9 o____ o____

5 ⭐⭐ **Choose the correct options.**

Crossing from
Chamonix to Italy

There are two main ways to get from Chamonix in France to Italy.

The quickest way is [1] **over / along / through** the Mont Blanc tunnel. You drive [2] **into / past / along** the tunnel just a short distance from Chamonix centre. The tunnel is 11.5km long and you come [3] **up / out of / through** the tunnel at Courmayeur in Italy.

However, there is a much more exciting (and expensive) way to make the journey. You can go [4] **through / over / along** the mountains in a special mountain car. You get on at Chamonix and go [5] **over / across / up** to an amazing 4000 metres at the Aiguille du Midi. A second car then takes you back [6] **down / out / over** to La Palud on the Italian side.

Don't go into Courmayeur. Drive [7] **past / over / across** the town and go another 35km [8] **through / along / across** the SS26 road to the beautiful town of Aosta, where you can get a delicious Italian ice cream or pizza.

Grammar summary

Past continuous and past simple with *while* and *when*

While I **was cooking** dinner, my sister **came** home with a pizza.

My sister **came** home with a pizza **while** I **was cooking** dinner.

I **was cooking** dinner **when** my sister **came** home with a pizza.

When my sister **came** home with a pizza, I **was cooking** dinner.

Wh- questions

Where **were** you **going when** I **saw** you?

What **were** you **doing when** the police **stopped** you?

Note

Usage

- We can use the past simple and the past continuous together to talk about an action that happened while another action was in progress.
- We use the past continuous for the longer action. We use the past simple for the shorter, finished action.
- We link the two tenses with *while* before the past continuous or *when* before the past simple.
  I saw Mark while I was walking to school.
  I was playing football when I hurt my leg.
- When we start the sentence with *when* or *while*, we link the two halves of the sentence with a comma.
  While I was eating, someone took my mobile phone.
  When I got home, my parents were watching television.

Common mistakes

~~When I was working, I fell asleep.~~ ✗
While I was working, I fell asleep. ✓
~~I was cycling while it started raining.~~ ✗
I was cycling when it started raining. ✓

5c A dog which bends.

Vocabulary: Types of film

1 ⭐ **Label the pictures with the words from the box.**

- action • crime • western
- science fiction • thriller • animated
- romance • musical • comedy • spy
- fantasy • horror

1 An action film

2 A _____

3 A _____

4 A _____

5 An _____ film

6 A _____

7 A _____ film

8 A _____

9 A _____ film

10 A _____ film

11 A _____ film

12 A _____ film

Grammar: Defining relative causes with *who, which* and *where*

2 ⭐ **Choose the correct options.**

1 This is a film **who / which** I really want to see.

2 Merida is the Disney Princess **where / who** I'd like to be!

3 Hollywood is the place **where / which** the best films come from.

4 It's a film about two men **which / who** find aliens.

5 I like films **where / which** make me laugh.

6 I know someone **which / who** has got 1000 films on DVD.

7 I went to the café **where / which** James Bond drank coffee.

8 Musicals are films **who / which** my mum loves.

9 My mum is a person **who / which** always cries when she watches sad films.

3 ⭐⭐ **Complete the sentences with *who, which* or *where*. Then complete the names with one letter in each space.**

1 It's a country *which* you get to through a wardrobe. _N a r n i a_

2 He's a boy _____ lives in a railway station. __ u __ __

3 It's the place _____ Neo really lives. The __ __ t __ __ x

4 He's a super-hero _____ works for a newspaper called *The Daily Bugle*. __ __ __ d __ __ – M __ __

5 It's a ship _____ hits an iceberg. __ __ t __ __ __ c

6 He's a schoolboy _____ plays a game called Quidditch. __ __ r __ y P __ __ __ e __

7 They are animals _____ live in an apartment in New York. Mr Popper's __ __ n __ __ __ n __

8 It's on an island _____ dinosaurs live. __ __ r __ s __ __ c __ __ r __

4 ★★★ Combine the two sentences with a relative clause to make one sentence.

1 Greg Heffley is a boy. He writes a diary.
   Greg Heffley is a boy who writes a diary.

2 Panem is a country. The Hunger Games take place there.
   _____

3 Pi is a man. He spends a long time on a boat with a tiger.
   _____

4 Pride Rock is a place. The Lion King lives there.
   _____

5 Toothless is a dragon. It is very friendly.
   _____

6 *The Unicorn* is a boat. Tintin and Captain Haddock want to find it.
   _____

7 Neverland is a country. Peter Pan took Wendy there.
   _____

8 Jumanji is a game. It is very dangerous to play it!
   _____

Use your English: Buy tickets at the cinema

5 ★ Complete the dialogue with the phrases from the box.

> • Here you   • Which performance   • I'd like
> • How much   • The 5.30   • £22 altogether

A: Hello, can I help you?

B: Yes. [1] *I'd like* four tickets to see the new Tintin film, please.

A: [2] _____? The 5.30 or the 7.45?

B: [3] _____, please.

A: Is that four adult tickets?

B: No, two adults and two children.

A: OK, that's fine.

B: [4] _____ is that?

A: That's [5] _____, please.

B: [6] _____ are.

A: Thank you. Enjoy the film.

Grammar summary

Defining relative causes with *who, which* and *where*
People (*who*)
These are the people **who** were in my film.   That's the boy **who** ate my burger!
Things (*which*)
It's a film **which** always makes me laugh.   I've got an idea **which** I think you'll like.
Places (*where*)
This is the place **where** Johnny Depp was born.   I want to live in a country **where** I can find a good job.

Note

Usage

- We use defining relative clauses to say which person, place or thing we are talking about. We need the clause for other people to understand what we are talking about.
- We use *who* to talk about people.
- We use *which* to talk about things.
- We use *where* to talk about places.
  He's an actor who I really admire.
  This is a place where you can relax.
  I'd like to see a film which really makes people think.

Common mistakes

~~They're the people which helped us.~~ ✗
They're the people who helped us. ✓
~~It's a place where I love.~~ ✗
It's a place which I love. ✓

1 **Complete the second sentence so that it has a similar meaning to the first.**

1 Paul is a very fast driver. Paul drives _very fast._

2 I'm not very good at singing.

I can't _____

_____.

3 Paul was playing football when he broke his leg.

While _____

_____.

4 I was waiting for my bus when Dad drove past.

Dad _____

_____.

5 It was easy for us to pass the exam.

We passed _____

_____.

6 The teacher was watching you when you sent that text.

You sent _____

_____.

7 While I was shopping, I lost my wallet.

I was _____

_____.

…/6

2 **Choose the correct options.**

I ¹ **was** / **were** looking in the local newspaper ² **while** / **when** I saw that there was a Horror Night at the cinema. I phoned a friend ³ **which** / **who** loves horror films and we decided to go. ⁴ **When** / **While** I was waiting for him, Melanie Hooper from my class walked ⁵ **along** / **past** me and went ⁶ **into** / **across** the cinema. My friend arrived and while he ⁷ **was** / **were** getting the tickets, I ⁸ **bought** / **buy** some popcorn. Then, we walked ⁹ **up** / **over** the stairs to the place ¹⁰ **which** / **where** the horror films were on. While we ¹¹ **waited** / **were waiting** for the film to start, Melanie sat next to me. During a bit in the film ¹² **which** / **who** was very frightening, Melanie held my arm. I didn't mind at all!

…/11

3 **Combine the two sentences to make one.**

1 I talked to a man. He knew Kate Winslett.

I _talked to a man who knew Kate Winslett._

2 I was taking photos. I dropped my camera.

While _____.

3 We were walking in the mountains. I fell and hurt my leg.

I _____.

4 We met a man. He was once in a Bond film.

We _____.

5 Sue hit another car. She was driving home.

While _____.

6 This is the restaurant. I told you about it.

This _____.

…/5

4 **Use the prompts to write sentences.**

1 I/walk/home yesterday/I/meet/Phil

I was walking home yesterday when I met Phil.

2 He's the boy/know/a lot about computers.

_____

3 I/meet/him/last week/near the café/you/work

_____

4 I/cycle/home yesterday/a bus/hit me

_____

5 It/be/the bus/take/us to school

_____

6 The man/drive/it/not see/me

_____

7 I get up/the driver/look/at me/nervously

_____

8 This is the place/Jack/have/his party

_____

9 I/arrive/he/sing

_____

10 Simon/make/a film of the party/we/go to/last week

_____

…/18

🎧 **LISTEN AND CHECK YOUR SCORE**

Total	…/40

5 Skills practice

SKILLS FOCUS: READING AND WRITING

Read

1 Read the text. When was the original Globe Theatre open?

a) 1599–1613

b) 1613–1642

c) 1599–1642

In 1599, a group of men, including William Shakespeare, decided to build a new theatre in Southwark, near the River Thames. They called it The Globe. Three thousand people watched plays in the theatre. The rich ones sat in seats. Others in the audience paid one penny and stood in front of the stage.

There was no lighting so plays took place in the afternoon. There were no microphones so the actors shouted their lines. The actors wore costumes and there were other things they could use. Things like cannons …

Unfortunately, in 1613, while the actors were performing *Henry VIII*, they fired the cannon and it started a fire in the roof. They opened a new Globe Theatre the next year but, in 1642, the government closed all theatres and that was the end of The Globe – until 1997 when the new Globe Theatre opened in almost the same place.

2 Read the text again and answer true (T), false (F) or doesn't say (DS).

1 The men who built The Globe were all actors.

   DS

2 There were three thousand seats in the theatre.

   _____

3 It cost one penny to stand and watch a play.

   _____

4 People watched plays in the afternoon. _____

5 Henry VIII closed the theatre in 1613. _____

Write

3 Complete the story with the words from the box.

   • in • ~~last~~ • next • suddenly • bit • at

¹ <u>Last</u> year, when we were in Italy, my mum bought some cheese to take home as a present. We left our apartment and said goodbye to the owner. ² _____ my mum realised that the cheese was still in the fridge. We ran back, but the owner wasn't there. Mum phoned him and a ³ _____ later he returned and we got the cheese. ⁴ _____ the evening, we went to the railway station and got on our train. The ⁵ _____ morning, we woke up in Rome and got off the train. We checked all our bags. ⁶ _____ first, we thought everything was OK and then, while we were walking to the taxis, my mum shouted: 'The cheese!'

4 Write a story about forgetting something. Use the time phrases from the story in Exercise 3.

6 IN TOWN

Vocabulary: Places in town

1 ⭐ **Match the places from the box to the reasons for going there (1–10).**

> • ~~zoo~~ • theatre • market • hospital
> • art gallery • travel agent • library
> • tourist information centre • museum
> • hotel

Where do people go …

1 to see animals? _zoo_

2 to see paintings? _____

3 when they are ill? _____

4 to sleep for the night? _____

5 to borrow books? _____

6 to see interesting old things? _____

7 to book a holiday? _____

8 for information about the place they are visiting? _____

9 to buy fresh fruit or other things? _____

10 to see a play? _____

2 ⭐⭐ **Complete the text with one letter in each space.**

My parents went to the travel [1] _a g e n t_ to book a holiday to Bruges in Belgium. Dad went to the petrol [2] s __ __ t __ __ __ for petrol and Mum went to the [3] l __ __ r __ r __ to borrow some books about the city.

Their [4] h __ __ __ l was near the town [5] h __ l __. Dad was worried about high prices so they stopped at a shopping [6] c __ __ t __ __ outside Bruges and bought some food. Dad got some maps from a [7] t __ u __ __ s __ information centre. On the second day, Dad lost his wallet. They went to the police [8] s __ __ t __ __ __ and someone brought the wallet in while they were there.

Grammar: Too + adjective (+ infinitive) and (not) + adjective + enough (+ infinitive)

3 ⭐ **Complete the sentences with too or enough.**

I like my town, but there are some problems:

1 The hotels are _too_ expensive.

2 The zoo is _____ small.

3 The theatre isn't big _____.

4 The hospital isn't clean _____.

5 My school is _____ difficult!

6 The market is _____ crowded.

However:

7 The streets are safe _____ to ride a bike to school.

8 The swimming pool is big _____ (and cheap _____) for me.

4 ⭐⭐ **Complete the second sentence so that it has the same meaning as the first. Use the word in capitals and too or enough.**

Homework: Describe your school.

Our school

1 Our school is too small. BIG
Our school isn't big enough.

2 The tests are too difficult. EASY
_The tests _____._

3 The lessons are too long. SHORT
_The lessons _____._

4 The homework isn't interesting enough.
BORING
_The homework _____._

5 The classrooms aren't warm enough.
COLD
_The classrooms _____._

6 … and I'm not old enough to leave!
YOUNG
_… and I'm _____._

This is not what I wanted. It is too short and not good enough. C-

5 ★★ Use the prompts to write sentences.

1

a) It/expensive/buy

It's too expensive to buy.

b) I/not rich/buy/it

_____

2

a) It/not modern/play games on

_____

b) It/old/play games on

_____

3

a) I/tall/sleep on this

_____

b) It/not long/sleep on

_____

4

a) It/difficult/do

_____

b) I/not clever/do this

_____

5

a) I/not hungry/eat all that

_____

b) It/big/eat

_____

Grammar summary

Too + adjective (+ infinitive) and not + adjective + enough (+ infinitive)

Too + adjective (+ infinitive)

It's **too far to walk**.
I'm **too tired to go out**.
We're **too late to see** the film.

(Not) + adjective + enough (+ infinitive)

My room **is big enough** for me.
My computer **isn't fast enough to play** games on.
My room **isn't tidy enough** for my mum!

Note

Usage

- We use *too* + adjective to say that there is more than we need or want. It explains what the problem is.
  The shopping centre is too crowded.
  My room is too small.
- We use *not* + adjective + *enough* to say that there is less than we need or want. It explains what the problem is.
  There isn't enough space in my bag.
  There aren't enough buses.
- We use adjective + *enough* to say that there is no problem.
  The swimming pool was big enough.
  I worked hard enough to pass my exams.

Common mistakes

~~The bed wasn't enough comfortable.~~ ✗
The bed wasn't comfortable enough. ✓

6b When's he arriving?

Phrases

1 ⭐⭐ **Complete the dialogue with the words from the box.**

- believe • with • bit • me • don't
- complicated • luck • ~~remind~~

A: So, do you remember our holiday plans?

B: Er … ¹ *Remind* ² _____ again. We're taking the ferry to France, right?

A: I ³ _____ ⁴ _____ it! We decided to go by plane – about three months ago.

B: Oh, right. Did we? Why?

A: Well, it's a ⁵ _____ ⁶ _____ but, basically, the ferry arrives too late for the train and the plane is actually slightly cheaper. We get to the airport at five o'clock in the evening and, ⁷ _____ a bit of ⁸ _____, we'll catch the 6.25 train to Nice.

B: Oh, now I remember. Dave told me. You get seasick. That's why it all changed!

Vocabulary: Transport

2 ⭐ **Label the pictures.**

1 s*hip*

2 s _____

7 c _____

6 h _____

3 f _____

5 v _____

4 m _____

3 ⭐ **Complete the words with one letter in each space.**

1 It's like 1 and 3 in Exercise 2

   b o a t

2 It's like 2 in Exercise 2 but bigger.

   __ __ t __ r __ __ k __

3 It's like 5 in Exercise 2 but much bigger.

   __ __ r __ y

4 It's like a bus, but you can go further on it.

   __ o __ c __

5 It's a bit like a bus and a bit like a train.

   __ r a __

6 You fly in it.

   __ l __ __ e

Grammar: Present continuous for future arrangements

4 ⭐ **Complete the text with the correct form of the verbs in brackets.**

Dear Sam,

Here are our holiday plans. We ¹ *'re taking* (take) the train to the airport at five past five on Monday afternoon. We ² _____ (stay) at an airport hotel on Monday night because we ³ _____ (fly) to Málaga very early in the morning.

On Wednesday we ⁴ _____ (take) a day trip to Tangier. The next day, Ben ⁵ _____ (go) whale watching. I'm going to relax in a café. We haven't got any plans for the rest of the week. We ⁶ _____ (return) on Sunday at 12.35 and on Sunday evening, we ⁷ _____ (go) to the theatre with Jo and Katy!

See you when we get back.

Lucy

5 ★★★ Use the prompts to write questions and answers. Then complete the diary entry below.

1 What/you/do/on Monday afternoon?

I/go/to the dentist

What are you doing on Monday afternoon?

I'm going to the dentist.

2 you/meet/Sam on Tuesday?

✗ I/meet/Jane on Tuesday

_____

_____

_____

3 When/play/tennis/with Louisa?

I/not/play/tennis with Louisa. I/play/golf with her on Wednesday

_____

_____

_____

4 you/have/a party on Thursday?

✗ I/have/a party on Friday. My grandparents/visit/us on Thursday

_____

_____

_____

_____

5 you/go/on holiday at the weekend?

✓ I /leave/on Saturday. I/stay/in London on Saturday night then/I/fly/to Greece on Sunday morning

_____

_____

_____

_____

MONDAY	1 *dentist* - p.m.
TUESDAY	2 _____
WEDNESDAY	3 _____
THURSDAY	4 _____
FRIDAY	5 _____
SATURDAY	Leave - 6 _____
SUNDAY	7 _____ - a.m.

Grammar summary

Present continuous for future arrangements

Affirmative	Negative
I'm **meeting** Jane on Tuesday.	I'm **not having** a party this year.
You're **leaving** tomorrow.	You **aren't staying** in London on Saturday.
He's/She's/It's **arriving** this evening.	He/She/It **isn't leaving** at seven.
We're/They're **having** a party on Friday.	We/They **aren't having** a test tomorrow.

Questions	Short answers
Are you **meeting** your friends later?	Yes, I **am**. No, I'm **not**.
Is she **getting** her hair cut tomorrow?	Yes, she **is**. No, she **isn't**.
Are they **eating** out on Saturday?	Yes, they **are**. No, they **aren't**.

Wh- questions
What **are** you **doing** this weekend?
How long **is** he **staying** with you?

Note

Usage

- We use the present continuous to talk about the future when there is an arrangement, usually with someone else.

  I'm meeting Tom later.

- Sometimes, it is possible to use either the present continuous or *going to*. The more definite the arrangement, the more natural it is to use the present continuous.

  We're going to meet outside the cinema.

  We're meeting outside the cinema.

Form

- We often use a future time expression with the present continuous to make it clear that we aren't talking about now.

  I'm having a party next week.

  We're leaving in the morning.

Common mistakes

- We can't use the present continuous to make future predictions.

  It's raining later. ✗

  It's going to rain later. ✓

6c I'd like a green salad, please.

Vocabulary: Restaurant food

1 [★] Complete the menu with one letter in each gap.

⟳ Menu ⟳

Meat
1 _l a m b_
2 k __ b __ b
3 chicken c __ __ __ y steak

Pasta
spaghetti bolognese
6 l __ __ __ g n __
7 __ __ v __ __ l __

Fish
fish soup
4 g __ __ l __ __ d
s __ __ d __ n __ __
salmon
5 p __ __ w __ __

Side orders
rice
salad (green, tomato)
8 g __ __ l __ c
b __ __ __ d
9 __ e __ s __ __ __ s
apple pie
ice cream
10 __ h __ __ __ s __ c __ __ __ e

Grammar: *Like* and *would like*

2 [★] Choose the correct questions or answers.

1 What food do you like?
 (a) I like fast food.   b) I'd like a steak, please.

2 Do you like cheese?
 a) No, I wouldn't.   b) No, I don't

3 a) Would you like some cake?
 b) Do you like cake?
 No, thank you. I'm not hungry.

4 Would you like a dessert?
 a) No, thank you.   b) Yes, I do.

5 What would you like for dessert?
 a) Cheesecake, please.
 b) Ice cream, apple pie, cheesecake. I like everything!

6 Are you ready to order?
 a) Yes, I like the chicken.
 b) Yes, I'd like the chicken.

7 a) Would you like some cola?
 b) Do you like cola?
 No, just some water, thank you.

3 [★★] Complete the dialogues with the correct form of *like* or *would like*.

A: Excuse me. Could I ask you some questions about your favourite foods?
B: Yes, of course.
A: Thank you. [1] (you/like) _Do you like_ fish?
B: [2] (✓) _____. I love it.
A: What desserts [3] (you/like) _____?
B: I [4] (✗ like) _____ desserts. I never eat them. My brother [5] (like) _____ ice cream. He [6] (✗ like) _____ vegetables or salad, but he loves sweet things.
A: Thank you.

Waiter: Good afternoon. What [7] (you/like) _____?
Woman: Er ... I [8] (like) _____ chicken curry, please.
Waiter: [9] (you/like) _____ any rice?
Woman: [10] (✓) _____, but not white rice. I [11] (like) _____ brown rice and a green salad, please.

4 [★★] Complete the questions.

1 A: _Would you like_ a drink?
 B: Yes, please. Water, please.

2 A: _____ your mum _____ curry?
 B: No, she doesn't. She hates it.

3 A: _____ your son _____ an ice cream?
 B: Yes, please, but just a small one.

4 A: What _____ you _____ for dinner?
 B: Meat or fish or sometimes some pasta with cheese.

5 A: _____ you _____ to go to the cinema this evening?
 B: No, I'm a bit tired today.

6 A: Where _____ you _____ to go this afternoon?
 B: Can we go to the park? That would be great.

Use your English: Order food in a restaurant

5 ⬚ **Complete the first part of the dialogue with the words from the box.**

> • have • can • ~~order~~ • too • me
> • anything • for • like • else

A: Good evening. Are you ready to [1] *order*?

B: Yes, we are. I'd [2] _____ a steak, please.

C: A chicken curry for [3] _____, please.

A: Anything [4] _____?

B: I'll [5] _____ a green salad, please.

C: Me [6] _____, please.

A: Would you like [7] _____ to drink?

B: [8] _____ I have a lemonade, please?

C: A mineral water [9] _____ me, please.

6 ⬚ **Complete the rest of the dialogue with one word in each gap.**

B: Thank you, that was lovely.

A: [1] W*ould* you like some dessert?

B: [2] N_____ for me, thanks. Would you [3] I_____ anything?

C: Yes, please. I'd like some cheesecake, please.

A: [4] A_____ else? Coffee?

B: No, that's [5] f _____, thanks. Can we have the [6] b _____, please?

A: Certainly. Here you are.

Grammar summary

Like and would like

Like: Affirmative	Negative
I **like** fish. He **likes** cheese.	They **don't like** curry. She **doesn't like** cola.
Questions	Short answers
Do you **like** tomatoes? **Does** she **like** cheesecake?	Yes, we **do**. No, we **don't**. Yes, she **does**. No, she **doesn't**

Would like

I'd like steak.	
Questions	Short answers
Would you **like** a drink?	Yes, we **would**. No, we **wouldn't**.
Wh- Questions	
What **would** you **like** to drink?	

Note

Usage

- We use *like* (+ verb + *-ing*) to talk about things we like and which are always true.
  I like kebabs.
  I like eating out.
- We use *would like* (+ *to* + infinitive) to talk about our preferences at this time.
  I'd like steak, please.
  I'd like to go home now.
  We use *Would* + subject + *like* (+ *to* + infinitive) to offer something to somebody or invite somebody to do something.
  Would you like a drink?
  Would you like to go swimming?

Form

- *Like* is a normal verb. We use the auxiliary *do* to form questions and negatives. We add *-s* to the third person singular in the present simple.
  Do you like cheese?
  My mum likes mushrooms.
- To make negatives with *would like,* we add *n't (not)* to *would.*
  You wouldn't like to go climbing.
- To form questions, we reverse the order of the subject and *would.*
  You would like to order now.
  Would you like to order now?

6 Language round-up

1 **Match the beginnings (1–9) to the endings (a–i).**

1 We're going to the shopping   a) station.

                   b) centre.

2 This is the new town

3 We can book a holiday at the travel   c) gallery.

        d) pie and cream.

4 Don't drive too fast past the police   e) salad.

5 I'd like a chicken   f) bread.

6 I'll have the green   g) agent.

7 I'd like some apple   h) curry.

8 Let's have some garlic   i) hall.

9 I love looking round the art

…/8

2 **Complete the text with the words from the box.**

> • like • would • meat • going • big
> • likes • having • too • desserts
> • expensive • orders • enough • salad

'I'd ¹ _like_ to have a meal and a disco for my birthday,' I said. Our house is ² _____ small and it wasn't special ³ _____ for me. The local hotel was too ⁴ _____, but the Italian restaurant was ⁵ _____ enough for all my friends and cheap.

Mum chose the food. She ⁶ _____ doing things like that. She chose lots of ⁷ _____ like kebabs, side ⁸ _____ of tomato ⁹ _____ and some great ¹⁰ _____ like cheesecake.

I wrote the invitations: 'Hi, I'm ¹¹ _____ a party on 26ᵗʰ June, ¹² _____ you like to come?' We're ¹³ _____ to the restaurant now to get everything ready. I hope it's a good night.

…/12

3 **Rearrange the letters to make four words for each heading.**

Places in town	Transport	Restaurant food
museum	_____	_____
_____	_____	_____
_____	_____	_____
_____	_____	_____

• ~~usmmeu~~ • ibinsum • hateret • npsraw
• slegana • avarnac • toscreo • seeacckeeh
• ribyarl • oplashti • iloviar • tophilrece

…/11

4 **Use the prompts to complete the dialogue.**

A: What/you/like/do/tomorrow?

1 _What would you like to do tomorrow?_

B: I/like/go/to the theatre. We can walk there.

2 _____ We can walk there.

A: It/far/walk

3 _____

B: OK, we can get a taxi.

A: I/not/rich/pay/for a taxi!

4 _____

B: We can ask your dad to take us.

A: He/work/tomorrow afternoon

5 _____

    Anyway, I/not/like/go/to the theatre

6 _____

B: Don't you?

A: No. Today, I/like/visit/the art gallery

7 No. _____

B: OK. you/like/meet/for lunch first?

8 OK. _____

A: Where? The tapas bar?

B: No. It/always/crowded/find/a table

9 No. _____

A: We can go to the Metro Bar.

B: Great. Their sandwiches/tasty/for me!

10 Great. _____

…/9

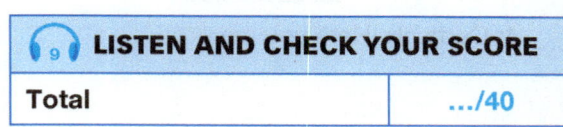

LISTEN AND CHECK YOUR SCORE

Total	…/40

6 Skills practice

SKILLS FOCUS: READING, LISTENING AND **WRITING**

Read

1 **Read the texts and answer N (Natasha), M (Mick) or J (Julia).**

Who...

1 would like to live in a different place? J

2 doesn't often go out in the evening? ___

3 can go to the theatre without spending much money? ___

4 spends two weeks' money on one trip to the cinema? ___

5 doesn't think their park is dangerous? ___

6 talks about a place for teenagers to go which isn't open now? ___

1

I don't like living here. The theatre has cheap tickets for students and there is a free art gallery, but I don't often go out in the evenings. The streets are too dark and the buses are too empty. I think it's quite dangerous to go out after dark.
Natasha

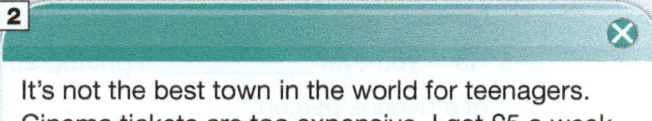

2

It's not the best town in the world for teenagers. Cinema tickets are too expensive. I get £5 a week from my parents and a ticket for the cinema costs £6. With bus tickets and popcorn it's £10 or more. My friends and I usually meet in the park. It's safe enough and free.
Mick

3

The youth club closed a few years ago. Now there's just one cinema and a big shopping centre. There are sometimes fights because teenagers are bored. I'd love to live in an exciting city like London, but my parents like it here because it's clean and houses are cheap.
Julia

Listen

2 🎧 **Listen to the dialogue. What is the problem?**

a) Rick doesn't know when the party is.

b) Beth doesn't want to go to his party.

c) Beth is too busy to go to his party.

3 🎧 **Listen again and complete the summary.**

Rick's party is on [1] *Friday*, but Beth is going to [2] _____ for the weekend. Next Friday, Beth is going to the [3] _____ with her aunt. After that, she is going to spend two days with her [4] _____. Beth has French classes on Mondays and [5] _____ and, on Thursdays, she plays [6] _____. Next Tuesday the [7] _____ club are having a meeting. Beth and Rick arrange to go out for a [8] _____ on Sunday evening at [9] _____ o'clock.

Write

4 **You and your friend went out for a meal at a restaurant. You left your phone there and, the next morning, a waiter from the restaurant returned it to you. Complete the thank you note to the manager.**

Dear Sir,

My [1] n *ame* is Filip Castro. I [2] w _____ at your restaurant [3] l _____ night and, at the end of the evening, I accidentally [4] l _____ my phone there. This morning, a waiter from your restaurant [5] c _____ to my home with the phone. It was very [6] k _____ of him to bring it. I'd [7] l _____ to thank you and him for your help.

The [8] m _____ was delicious and I will definitely come back to your restaurant soon. Thank you again.

Filip Castro

Vocabulary: Holiday activities

1 ⭐ Rearrange the letters to make holiday activities.

In the mountains

1 g / l / n / i / c / i / b / m
climbing

2 n / o / a / n / m / u / t / i   n / k / i / b / i / g
_____

3 i / i / g / n / k / s
_____

4 g / r / o / a / n / b / n / s / w / o / i / d
_____

In the sea

5 g / w / n / m / i / i / s / m
_____

6 n / n / i / i / f / d / w / s / r / u / g
_____

On the beach

7 h / n / i / t / n / b / g / u / s / a
_____

8 a / h / e / c / b   l / a / o / b / l / v / l / y / e / l
_____

In the town

9 g / h / n / o / s / i / p / p
_____

10 s / t / g / e / i / e / h / g / s / i / n
_____

Grammar: The definite article with places

2 ⭐ Complete the text with *the* or –.

DREAM HOLIDAYS

I love looking at travel magazines and websites and I've now got a list of places I want to visit when I get older.

[1] *The* USA. I want to see [2] _____ Los Angeles and [3] _____ New York. I want to go to [4] _____ Rocky Mountains and go on a boat trip along [5] _____ Mississippi River ... and there are lots of other places I want to go to as well.
[6] _____ Africa. I want to see

Grammar: Present perfect simple with *ever* and *never*

3 ⭐ Write the past participle of the verbs. Circle the verbs which are the same in the past simple and the present perfect.

1 put	*put*	9 give	_____
2 have	_____	10 come	_____
3 swim	_____	11 drive	_____
4 meet	_____	12 sleep	_____
5 speak	_____	13 fly	_____
6 eat	_____	14 do	_____
7 break	_____	15 see	_____
8 take	_____		

4 ⭐⭐ Complete the sentences with the correct past participles from Exercise 3.

1 Have you ever *done* the ironing?
2 I've never _____ a car.
3 Have you ever _____ to someone on Skype?
4 Have you ever _____ the Pyramids?
5 I've never _____ curry.
6 Has your dad ever _____ a plane?
7 My mum has never _____ in an ocean.
8 Have you ever _____ a photograph of a famous person?

[7] _____ Sahara Desert and ride on a camel. I want to go on a boat ride on [8] _____ River Nile and I want to swim in [9] _____ Red Sea and look at the fish.
[10] _____ Canary Islands. I want to swim in [11] _____ Atlantic Ocean and see the black sand on Lanzarote.

5 ⭐⭐ Use the prompts to write sentences.

1 My dad/go to Paris ✓/but/climb the Eiffel Tower ✗

My dad has been to Paris, but he's never climbed the Eiffel Tower.

2 I/go/to Spain ✓/but/swim/in the Mediterranean ✗

_____

_____

3 My parents/eat/Chinese food ✓/but/visit China ✗

_____

_____

4 My aunt/go/to the mountains ✓/but/go skiing ✗

_____

_____

5 My friends/ride/a motorbike ✓/but/drive a car ✗

_____

_____

6 My teacher/do/lots of interesting things ✓/but/ she/see/a horror film ✗

_____

_____

6 ⭐⭐⭐ Use the prompts to write questions and answers.

1 you/ever/eat/a full English breakfast? ✓

Have you ever eaten a full English breakfast? Yes, I have.

2 your dad/ever/play/beach volleyball? ✗

_____

_____

3 you/ever/go/to the British Museum? ✗

_____

_____

4 your mum/ever/ride/a mountain bike? ✓

_____

_____

5 your grandparents/ever/write/an email? ✓

_____

_____

6 your sister/ever/break/her arm? ✗/but/she/break/her leg twice

_____

_____

Grammar summary

The definite article with places

The USA

The River Nile

The Himalayas

The Red Sea

The Faroe Islands

The Sahara Desert

Note

- We use the definite article to talk about plural countries, groups of mountains, rivers, seas, oceans, groups of islands and deserts. We do not use it with singular countries, individual mountains or islands or lakes.
  The USA but NOT ~~The England~~
  The Himalayas but NOT ~~The Everest~~
  The Canary Islands but NOT ~~The Lanzarote~~
  The River Nile but NOT ~~The Lake Victoria~~

Present perfect simple with *ever* and *never*

I**'ve (have) never been** to America.

He**'s (has) never eaten** lasagne.

Have you **ever forgotten** somebody's birthday?
Yes, I **have.**/No, I **haven't**.

Has she **ever seen** Niagara Falls?
Yes, she **has.**/No, she **hasn't**.

Note

Usage

- We use the present perfect simple with *ever* and *never* to talk about things that have or haven't happened in our lives.
  I have never been to Italy. (in my life)

Form

- To form the present perfect simple we use *have/has* + past participle.
  I stopped. I have stopped.
- To form questions, we reverse the order of *have/ has* and the subject.
  You have finished. Have you finished?
- We write *never* between *have/has* and the past participle.
  I have never failed an exam.
- We write *ever in* questions between the subject and the past participle.
  Have you ever driven a car?

7b It hasn't arrived yet.

Phrases

1 **Complete the dialogue with one word in each gap.**

A: Have you finished your homework yet?

B: Er … nearly.

A: You ¹ *mean* you haven't started yet. Hurry up. We can't go out until you've finished. Honestly, it's always the same. You never do your homework when Mum tells you to.

B: ² C _____ d _____. We've got all day. We can go out this afternoon.

A: Yes, but the ³ t _____ is that it's going to rain this afternoon.

B: Really? Does Mum know? I'm sure I can do my homework later. What do you ⁴ r _____?

A: No, way! She's already told you to finish your homework three times. She isn't going to change her mind now.

Grammar: Present perfect with *just, already* and *yet*

2 **Rewrite the underlined sentences with the words in capitals.**

1 A: You're brown.

B: I know. <u>I've come back from Greece.</u> JUST

I've just come back from Greece.

2 A: Can you tell me the answer to number two?

B: <u>I've told you the answer.</u> You weren't listening. ALREADY

_____

3 A: Let's go. B: We can't. <u>Jason isn't here.</u> YET

_____

4 A: Rob, <u>I've heard the news about your accident.</u> Are you alright? JUST

_____

5 A: <u>Has Tom given you your phone back?</u>

B: No, he hasn't. YET

_____

6 A: Quick! I don't want to miss the start of the film.

B: <u>You've missed it.</u> ALREADY

_____

3 **Choose the correct options.**

1 Don't stand up. The plane hasn't stopped **yet** / **already** / **just**.

2 I don't want to go to bed. The match hasn't finished **already** / **just** / **yet**.

3 'You look tired.' 'I am. I've **already** / **just** / **yet** got back from Australia.'

4 Have you read the email I sent you **already** / **yet** / **just**?

5 'Sir, what exercise do you want us to do?' 'I've **just** / **yet** / **already** told you three times.'

6 Has Helen phoned **yet** / **already** / **just**?

4 **Complete the email with the phrases from the box.**

- hasn't told - 've already done - haven't sent
- has just come - 've already paid
- have swum - haven't tried

Hi Sara,

I'm in Sennen in Cornwall. It's great here. ¹ We<u>'ve already done</u> lots of things.

We ² _____ in the sea every day, but I ³ _____ surfing yet. I'm going to have a lesson tomorrow. I ⁴ _____ so I hope it doesn't rain tomorrow!

Dad ⁵ _____ into the living room of our cottage. He wants to use the computer. Don't worry, he ⁶ _____ me to stop using it yet – he's making a cup of coffee first. I ⁷ _____ any postcards yet, but I'm going to buy some tomorrow.

See you soon.

Meg

5 ★★★ Use the prompts to complete the dialogues. Use *just*, *already* or *yet*.

1 A: The new James Bond film is great. I love the bit where …

   B: Don't tell me. (I/not/see it) *I haven't seen it yet*.

2 A: Do you want to see my holiday photos?

   B: No, thanks. (I/see/them twice!)

   _____

3 A: What's wrong with you?

   B: (I/see/an alien!)

   _____

4 A: What did I get in my test, sir?

   B: (I/not/look/at them)

   _____.

   I've been very busy.

5 A: (you/finish/Exercise 1,/Paul?)

   _____

   B: Not yet, sir.

Use your English: Exclamations

6 Choose the correct response.

1 Steve remembered to bring all his books to school today.

   a) What a surprise!   b) That's a pity!

   c) How horrible!

2 I've passed all my exams.

   a) How weird!   b) That's great!

   c) What a nightmare!

3 My parents say I can't go out for three weeks.

   a) What a nightmare!   b) That's odd!

   c) How nice!

4 Joe doesn't want to go out with me.

   a) What a fantastic idea!   b) That's a shame!

   c) That's good!

5 Our teacher left the classroom in the middle of the lesson.

   a) That's a shame!   b) What a nightmare!

   c) How strange!

6 My parents gave me a new laptop.

   a) That's incredible!   b) That's a shame!

   c) How disgusting!

Grammar summary

Present perfect with *just*, *already* and *yet*

I**'ve just got** home.

He**'s just left**.

They**'ve already done** the washing-up.

She**'s already arrived** in the USA.

I **haven't talked** to her **yet**.

It **hasn't started yet**.

Have you **finished yet**?

Has he **asked** you out **yet**?

Note

Usage

- We use the present perfect simple with *just* to talk about something that happened a very short time ago. *We've just finished dinner.*

- We use the present perfect simple with *already* to emphasise that something has happened before now. *I've already done the washing-up.*

- We use the present perfect simple with *yet* in questions and negatives to mean *up to now*. *Have you sent that email yet? He hasn't fallen asleep yet.*

Form

- We put *just* between the auxiliary verb *have/has* and the past participle. *He has just phoned.*

- We put *already* between the auxiliary verb *have/has* and the past participle. *I have already seen this film.*

- We put *yet* at the end of questions and negatives. *I haven't had a shower yet. Has Mark eaten his lunch yet?*

Common mistakes

He's left already. ✗

He's already left. ✓

7c He sang a rock song.

Vocabulary: Types of music

1 **Rearrange the letters to make the types of music.**

MUSIC SURVEY:

Write your musical likes and dislikes below.

Likes		Dislikes	
1	opp <u>pop</u>	8	zajz _____
2	par _____	9	atLni _____
3	eergag _____	10	kofl _____
4	okrc _____	11	ousl _____
5	eohtcn _____	12	lcaascisl _____
6	ihp-pho _____	13	rtocuny and nsrteew _____
7	yveha emlta _____		

Grammar: Past simple and present perfect simple

2 **Complete the sentences with the correct form of the verbs in brackets.**

1 I (go) _have been_ to America three times.

2 I (go) _____ to Spain last year.

3 (you ever meet) _____ any famous people?

4 (you meet) _____ any nice people when you were in England?

5 Where (Mark go) _____ yesterday?

6 Where (Mark go) _____? I can't find him.

7 I (just finish) _____ my homework.

8 I (finish) _____ my homework two minutes ago.

9 Rachel (send) _____ me two emails yesterday.

10 Rachel (send) _____ two emails so far this morning.

11 I (not do) _____ my homework last week.

12 I (not do) _____ my homework yet.

3 **Complete the texts with the verbs from the box.**

Elvis Presley
in concert
21st August
8.30 p.m.
Tickets: £3.50

JUSTIN BIEBER LIVE!
12th May
7.30 p.m.

- started (x2) • has been • have seen
- sold • has sung • has played
- saw • was • made • haven't been
- has sold • has appeared • played

Elvis Presley [1] _started_ his career in 1954 and [2] _____ a singer until he died in 1977. In that time he [3] _____ millions of records all over the world. He [4] _____ thirty-three films and [5] _____ concerts for his fans, but only in the USA and Canada. My mum [6] _____ him in concert three times and she [7] _____ to his house in Memphis twice.

Justin Bieber [8] _____ singing in 2008. He [9] _____ some good songs and he [10] _____ over fifteen million CDs and music downloads. He [11] _____ concerts all over the world and he [12] _____ in films and television programmes. I [13] _____ him in concert twice, but I [14] _____ to his house yet!

4 ★★★ Use the prompts to complete the dialogues.

1 A: ¹ you/ever/go/to a music festival?

Have you ever been to a music festival?

B: ² ✗ but I/go/to a pop concert

_____

_____

A: Really? When?

B: ³ I/see/Robbie Williams last year

_____

A: ⁴ you/enjoy it?

_____

B: ⁵ ✓ It/be/great

_____

2 A: ⁶ your brother's band/make/any CDs?

_____

_____

B: ⁷ ✗ Not yet.

_____

A: ⁸ they/play/any concerts?

_____

B: ⁹ ✓ They/play/last night

_____

_____

A: Really? ¹⁰ you/go?

_____

B: ¹¹ ✓ but they/not/be/very good

_____

3 A: ¹² your parents/ever/go/to a rock concert?

_____

_____

B: ¹³ ✓ They/go/to a lot/when they/be/younger

_____

_____

A: Really?

B: Yes. ¹⁴ They/see/U2 in 1990

_____

A: ¹⁵ they/enjoy it?

_____

B: ¹⁶ ✗

_____

Grammar summary

Past simple and present perfect simple

I**'ve seen** this film.
I **saw** this film last week.
He**'s been** to the USA.
He **went** to the USA two years ago.
I**'ve never eaten** Chinese food.
I **didn't eat** Chinese food when I was in Hong Kong.
He **hasn't done** his homework yet.
He **didn't do** his homework yesterday.
Have you **ever ridden** a camel?
Did you **ride** a camel when you were in Egypt?
Has she **ever had** a job?
Did she **have** a job last summer?

Note

Usage

- We use the past simple with a past time expression to talk about something that started and finished in the past. The time period has finished.
  We went out last Friday.
- We use the present perfect simple when the time period is unfinished or with time expressions such as *just, already, yet.*
  I've never seen this film. (in my life)
  We've been to the USA. (at some time in our life)
  They've just finished the washing-up.
- Some time expressions may be finished or unfinished depending on when we use them.
  I had French this morning. (It is now the afternoon or evening.)
  I've had three lessons this morning. (It is still the morning.)

Common mistakes

~~Did you ever go to the USA?~~ ✗
Have you ever been to the USA? ✓
~~What have you done yesterday?~~ ✗
What did you do yesterday? ✓

7 Language round-up

1 Match the beginnings (1–10) to the endings (a–j)

1	Have you ever	a)	arrived.
2	I've never	b)	Canada.
3	Bob has just	c)	yet.
4	I haven't finished	d)	USA.
5	Have you started	e)	last night?
6	We arrived	f)	seen a dolphin?
7	My dad's been to the	g)	out.
8	My mum has never been to	h)	yet?
9	Did you enjoy the concert	i)	ten minutes ago.
10	My mum's gone	j)	been here before.

.../9

2 Complete the dialogue with the correct form of the verbs from the box or *never, yet, already, just*.

> • write (x2) • be • do (x3) • ~~have~~

Erin: Are you ready to go out?

Tricia: I haven't [1] *had* dinner [2] _____ because I've [3] _____ got back from school. There [4] _____ a basketball match.

Erin: [5] _____ you play well?

Tricia: I was OK, but we aren't very good. We've [6] _____ won a game. It was 14–58 today! Anyway, I can't go out. I haven't [7] _____ my homework yet. Our English teacher has [8] _____ given us three pages of exercises to do. Haven't you got any homework?

Erin: I've [9] _____ done it. I [10] _____ it at lunch time. Phone me when you've finished. I can write some emails. Natalie [11] _____ to me last week and I haven't [12] _____ back to her yet.

Tricia: OK. See you later.

.../11

3 Write the words in capitals in the correct places.

1 MOUNTAIN JUST WENT THE

just   *the*   *went*   *mountain*

I've/got back from/Alps. I/climbing and/biking. It was incredible.

2 GO NEVER REGGAE THE

I've been to Caribbean. It's too expensive for me. I'd like to swimming and listen to music.

3 EVER BEEN WENT THE

Have you seen River Nile? My dad to Egypt ten years ago, but I've never there.

4 THE ALREADY THE

When we went to USA, we swam in Pacific Ocean near Los Angeles. I loved it. I've started planning next year's holiday!

.../11

4 Complete the text with one word in each space.

Dear Grandma and Grandpa,

We've [1] *been* here in France for a week now. We're staying in a campsite near [2] _____ Loire River. It's beautiful. Have you [3] _____ been here? You'd like it.

The people in the next tent are very noisy. They play heavy [4] _____ music all evening. Dad wants to play his country and [5] _____ CDs very loudly, but he hasn't done it [6] _____. (Mum says he can't!)

Yesterday, we [7] _____ to a town on [8] _____ Atlantic Ocean and I went windsurfing. I've [9] _____ tried it before so it was difficult.

Mum and Dad have [10] _____ shopping, but they'll be back soon.

Hope all is well.

Love,

Josh

.../9

🎧 **LISTEN AND CHECK YOUR SCORE**

Total	.../40

7 Skills practice

SKILLS FOCUS: READING AND WRITING

Read

1 **Read the text. Why is Masbat popular with young people?**

Most people who want to visit the Red Sea go to the resorts of Hurghada or Sharm el-Sheikh.

Another place which is less well-known is Dahab, north of Sharm el-Sheikh. There are three parts to Dahab. Masbat is a Bedouin village which has always been popular with young people who want a cheap holiday in the sun. It's a very relaxing place with a beach and the cafés play rock and reggae music. Mashraba is where the hotels are and where richer people stay. Medina is a great place for windsurfing.

One reason for coming to Dahab is the Blue Hole. This is a great place to see fish and go diving, but it is also very dangerous. The Hole is 130 metres deep and, 52 metres below the surface, there is a 26 metre long tunnel. The problem is that it is dangerous for inexperienced divers to go more than 40 metres down, but a lot of people want to reach the tunnel to see what it is like.

2 **Read the text again and match the places from the box to the descriptions (1–4).**

- Mashraba • ~~Hurghada~~ • the Blue Hole
- Masbat • Sharm el-Sheikh

1 Two popular Red Sea holiday resorts.
   Hurghada _____

2 A Bedouin village. _____

3 The part of Dahab where there are hotels.
   _____

4 A place where people go diving. _____

Write

3 **Complete the invitation with the extra information (A–E).**

- ~~A They've got a great house near the sea.~~
- B My aunt is a great cook. • C It isn't far.
- D They've got a few animals.
- E He worked on a ferry for ten years.

Dear Clara,

We're going to the Isle of Wight next weekend. My cousins live there. 1 *A* Would you like to come with us?

We're going to drive to Portsmouth. 2 ___

Then we get the ferry to the Isle of Wight. It's small, but it doesn't matter. It only takes twenty minutes to get there from Portsmouth.

My aunt and uncle live on a farm. 3 ___ I love going there because I like helping my uncle. They've also got a boat. My uncle knows a lot about the sea. 4 ___ Oh, and the food is delicious. 5 ___

So, do you want to come? Phone me or send me an email.

Belinda

4 **Write an invitation. Use the ideas below.**

A school friend is having a party on Friday. Write an invitation to your neighbour.

- Say who the school friend is – add extra information about his/her character.
- Say what time it starts and finishes – add extra information about how you are planning to get there.
- Say where the school friend lives – add extra information about his/her house.
- Tell your friend what you are going to wear – add extra information about when and where you bought the clothes.

8 JUST IMAGINE

Vocabulary: Personality adjectives

1 ⭐ **Complete the adjectives with one letter in each space.**

1 Chris always does well at school. He is very _c l e v e r_.

2 Beth always tells people what to do. She's quite b __ __ s __ .

3 Lisa never does much work. She's l __ __ y.

4 Frank always smiles and says hello. He's nice and f __ __ __ n __ __ y.

5 Meg never gives her friends presents. She's quite m __ __ n.

6 Fiona always makes us laugh. She's so f __ __ __ y.

7 Steve finds it hard to talk to people. He's very __ h __ .

8 Brian thinks he's better than anyone else. He's too __ i __ – h __ __ d __ d.

2 ⭐⭐ **Complete the crossword.**

Someone who …

1 always supports their friends is …

2 gives gifts to other people is …

3 makes you feel slightly angry is …

4 gives help to others is …

5 behaves or speaks nicely is …

6 is the opposite of (5) is …

7 doesn't say much is …

8 is messy is …

Grammar: Zero conditional with *if*

3 ⭐ **Complete the sentences with the correct form of the verbs in brackets.**

1 If we (have) _have_ a test, our teacher always (watch) _watches_ us carefully!

2 If I (not get) _____ up at seven o'clock, my mum (get) _____ very angry.

3 If my mum (work) _____ late, my dad (cook) _____ dinner.

4 If we (talk) _____ in class, our teacher (give) _____ us extra homework.

5 If I (not feel) _____ well, my mum (give) _____ me an onion and sugar drink.

6 If my brother (not understand) _____ his homework, he always (ask) _____ me for help.

4 ⭐ **Use the prompts to complete the questions.**

1 (What/your mum/do) _What does your mum do_ if you get bad marks from school?

2 (What music/you/listen to) _____ _____ if you are sad?

3 (Who/you/talk to) _____ _____ if you have problems?

4 (What/your dad/say) _____ _____ if you are late home?

5 (Where/you/go) _____ _____ if you want to be alone?

6 (How/you/get to school) _____ _____ if you miss the bus?

7 (What time/you/get up) _____ _____ if you don't have school?

8 (Where/you/stay) _____ _____ if you are on holiday?

5 ⭐⭐ **Look at the photos and complete the sentences with the correct form of the verbs from the box.**

> • come̶ • be (x3) • help (x2) • turn
> • take • fi̶g̶h̶t̶ • not know • lose • wear

1 If aliens _come_, he _fights_ them.

2 If he _____ the ring, people _____ he is there.

3 If he _____ angry, he _____ green.

4 If there _____ a crime, he _____ the police.

5 If he _____ his boat, he _____ a different one.

6 If there _____ dangerous spies, he _____ the goverment.

Grammar summary

Zero conditional with *if*

If I **finish** my homework early, I usually **surf** the internet.

If my mum **is** late, she always **phones** us.

If I **don't feel** well, I **go** to bed.

If my dad **is** angry, he **doesn't talk** to us.

Questions	Short answers
If it **rains**, **do** you **go** to school by car?	Yes, I **do**. No, I **don't**.

Wh- questions

What **do** you **do if** you **are** tired?

Where **does** your mum **go if** she **has** a night out with her friends?

> **Note**
>
> **Usage**
> - We use the zero conditional to talk about the result of a situation. The condition is always true.
>   *If I am late for school, my teacher contacts my parents.*
>   *(This always happens when I am late for school.)*
>
> **Form**
> - To form the zero conditional, we use *if* + present simple (action or situation) + present simple (result). The *if* clause can come at the beginning or end of the sentence. When it comes at the beginning of the sentence, we put a comma after it.
>   *If I have time in the evening, I phone my friends.*
>   *I phone my friends in the evening if I have time.*

8b Will life be different?

Grammar: *Will* for future predicitons

1 Use the prompts to complete the sentences.

In fifty years' time robots …

1 cook for us ✓
will cook for us.

2 clean the floor ✓
_____

3 do our homework ✗
_____

4 drive cars ✗
_____

5 tidy our rooms ✓
_____

6 teach us ✓
_____

7 wear clothes ✗
_____

8 do the washing-up ✓
_____

2 Use the prompts to write questions and short answers.

In 2050 …

1 children/go to school? ✓
Will children go to school? Yes, they will.

2 we/have flying cars? ✗ _____
_____

3 people/live in big cities? ✓ _____
_____

4 the world/be warmer? ✓ _____
_____

5 people/live on different planets? ✗ _____
_____

6 people/travel in space? ✓ _____
_____

7 people/eat meat? ✓ _____
_____

8 cars/use petrol? ✗ _____
_____

3 Complete the text with the correct form of the verbs from the box.

• be (x2) • go • return • try • disappear
• not listen • become • win • drive
• not kill • attack • destroy • live

What will happen
IN THE FUTURE?

Science fiction films often look at the future and here are some of the ideas about the future of the Earth.
There [1] *will be* a terrible natural disaster. Storms [2] _____ cities like New York and the Statue of Liberty [3] _____ under the ocean. We [4] _____ in modern houses, we [5] _____ flying cars and we [6] _____ to the moon for our holidays! Aliens [7] _____ the Earth. They [8] _____ stronger and more intelligent than us but they [9] _____ us all. We [10] _____ in the end and they [11] _____ to their planet. Robots [12] _____ intelligent. They [13] _____ to us and they [14] _____ to rule the world! So what do you think? What will the world be like in the future? Send us your ideas today.

Vocabulary: The weather

4 ⭐ Complete the dialogues with one word in each gap.

1
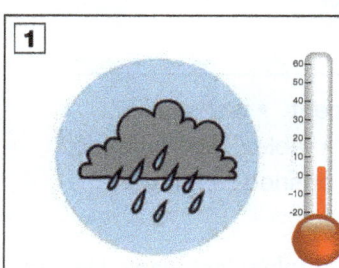
A: What is the w*eather* like today?
B: Terrible. It's r*aining* and it's c*old*.

2

A: See you later.
B: Drive carefully. It's very f_____ outside.

3
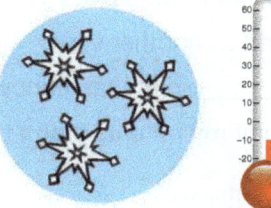
A: Mummy, it's s_____. Can I go outside?
B: Put a coat and hat on. It's f_____ out there.

4

A: What was the weather l_____ in Spain?
B: Brilliant! It was s_____ every day and very h_____.

5

A: Is the sun s_____ today?
B: No, it's c_____, but it's quite w_____ and at least it isn't raining.

6

A: Put your hat on.
B: Why?
A: It's very w_____ today.

Grammar summary

Will for future predicitons

Affirmative	Negative
We **will live** in skyscrapers. There **will be** a lot of problems.	People **won't go** to Mars. We **won't have** robots.
Questions	**Short answers**
Will people **use** electricity?	Yes, they **will**. No, they **won't**.

Wh- questions
How many people **will live** on Earth? What **will** we **eat**?

Note

Usage
- We use *will* to talk about things we think or believe will happen in the future.
  People will live to 150 years old.

Form
- In affirmative and negative sentences, we use *will* or *won't* + infinitive without *to*.
  You will get a good job.
  I won't get married.
- In questions, we reverse the order of the subject and the auxiliary verb *will*.
  We will go to the moon.
  Will we go to the moon?
- In short answers, we don't repeat the main verb.
  Will you leave England?
  Yes, I will. NOT ~~Yes, I will leave.~~

Common mistakes
~~Where I will live?~~ ✗
Where will I live? ✓

8c If you take too long, I'll ...

Phrases

1 ⭐ **Complete the dialogue with one word in each gap.**

A: I'm here at last. I'm really sorry I'm late. Do you think we can still get tickets for the concert?

B: [1] L*et's* h*ope* so. You wait here. I'll go and see.

A: [2] A_____ I_____?

B: No. They sold the last one five minutes ago.

A: [3] H_____ a_____. I'm sorry I wasn't here. Oh, why didn't I leave earlier?

B: Just [4] f_____ a_____ it. Come on. We've got £10 that we didn't spend on tickets. Let's go shopping.

Vocabulary: Computer language

2 ⭐ **Label the picture.**

1 l*aptop*

2 p_____

3 p_____

4 s_____

5 c_____

6 m_____ s _____

7 k_____

8 m_____

3 ⭐⭐ **Complete the text with the words from the box.**

- software • attachment • website
- password • virus • ~~tablet~~ • downloaded
- crashed • stick • opened • internet

My brother got a new [1] *tablet* last week. He connected it to the [2] _____ and set up his email account. Then he got a strange email with an [3] _____. He [4] _____ it and got a [5] _____ from it. His tablet [6] _____ – on the first day! Luckily, Dad had some anti-virus [7] _____ on a memory [8] _____ and he cleaned it. Then my brother found a [9] _____ with free games. He [10] _____ one and ... another virus! Dad's put a [11] _____ on the tablet now so my brother can't use it if my parents aren't there.

Grammar: First conditional with *if*

4 ⭐ **Match the beginnings (1–8) to the endings (a–h).**

1 If you get a bad virus,

2 If you get a tablet,

3 If you don't want these photos,

4 If you don't write any emails,

5 If you use your name as your password,

6 If your printer doesn't work,

7 If you can't find your charger,

8 If you press the caps lock button on your keyboard,

a) you won't receive any.

b) I'll take it to the shop for you.

c) YOU WILL WRITE IN CAPITAL LETTERS!

d) your computer will crash.

e) it won't be safe.

f) your phone won't work.

g) it will be easy to carry.

h) I'll delete them.

5 ★★ Use the prompts to complete the dialogues.

A: [1] (What/you/do) _What will you do_ if

[2] (Paul/be/late) _____ again?

[3] (you/wait) _____ for him?

B: [4] (✗) _____. [5] (If/he/be/late)

_____ again, [6] (I /phone/him)

_____ and tell him to meet me

inside the cinema.

A: [7] (Where/you/go) _____ if

[8] (it/be/sunny) _____ this

weekend? [9] (you/go) _____ to the

beach?

B: [10] (✓) _____.

[11] (If it/be/warm enough) _____

[12] (I/go/swimming) _____

Use your English: Describe and deal with computer problems

6 ★ Complete the dialogues with one word in each space.

A: Good morning. What's the [1] p_roblem_?

B: There's something [2] w _____ with my

tablet.

A: What's the [3] m _____ with it?

B: It doesn't [4] w _____.

A: [5] S _____ I have a look at it?

B: Yes, please. That [6] w _____ be great.

A: What's wrong, Shelley?

B: I've got a [7] p _____ with my charger.

A: What's wrong [8] w _____ it?

B: It doesn't charge my phone!

A: I'll [9] l _____ you my charger.

B: Thanks. That's really [10] k _____ of you.

Grammar summary

First conditional with *if*

If your computer **goes** wrong, **I'll look** at it for you.

If you **send** James an email, he**'ll write** back to you.

If you **don't clean** your keyboard, it **won't work** properly.

If this virus checker **doesn't work**, it **won't remove** the viruses.

Questions	Short answers
Will you **help** me **if** I **have** any problems?	Yes, I **will**. No, I **won't**.
Wh- questions	
Who **will** you **ask if** you **need** help with your new phone?	

Note

Usage

- We use the first conditional to talk about the result of a likely future event or situation.

  If it rains tomorrow (the likely situation), I'll stay in bed. (the result)

Form

- We form the first conditional with two clauses, the *if* clause and the result clause. We use *If* + present simple + *will* + infinitive without *to*.

  If you are late, I'll wait in the café.

- When we use the *if* clause first, we separate the two clauses with a comma. When we start with the result clause, we don't use a comma.

  If I see a cheap tablet, I'll buy it.

  I'll buy a tablet if it is cheap.

Common mistakes

~~If we will drive, it will be quicker.~~ ✗

If we drive, it will be quicker. ✓

8 Language round-up

1 Complete the sentences with the words from the box.

- tempered • working • headed • ~~annoying~~
- shining • going • email • internet • DVD
- crashed • stick

1 My brother is really _annoying_.
2 The sun is _____.
3 My sister is quite big- _____.
4 My computer has just _____.
5 My dad is often bad- _____.
6 You need a memory _____.
7 My best friend is very easy- _____.
8 I don't know how to burn this onto a _____.
9 I spend a lot of time surfing the _____.
10 I think I am quite hard- _____.
11 I want to attach a photo to this _____.

.../10

2 Complete the sentences with the correct form of the verbs in brackets.

1 I think you (be) _will be_ interested in my family.
2 If I have a problem, my mum always (help) _____ me.
3 If I do something wrong, she (not shout) _____.
4 If there (be) _____ a problem, my dad (not talk) _____ about it.
5 My brother is lazy. If my mum (not tell) _____ him to tidy his room or do his homework, he (not do) _____ it.
6 If you want to know more about us, I (tell) _____ you.
7 I (not have) _____ much time in May because we will have exams.

.../8

3 Complete the text with the correct form of the words in brackets.

When I woke up, it was [1] (cloud) _cloudy_, so I switched on my computer. At first, there was no [2] (connect) _____ to the internet, but later I received three emails. One had an [3] (attach) _____. I wanted to print it, but my [4] (print) _____ wasn't working. My brother wasn't very [5] (help) _____. He was looking for his [6] (charge) _____. He's very [7] (tidy) _____ and he can never find anything. He's also very [8] (annoy) _____ and says that I'm [9] (boss) _____.

It was [10] (sun) _____ after lunch, so I went cycling. Later, it was [11] (wind) _____ and difficult to cycle. Then it started raining …

.../10

4 Use the prompts to write questions and answers.

1 What/you do/if it/be/sun/tomorrow?
If it/be/sun/tomorrow/I/go/for a walk
What will you do if it is sunny tomorrow?
If it is sunny tomorrow, I'll go for a walk.

2 Where/we/go/if/it/rain/tomorrow?
If/it rain/tomorrow/we/go/to a museum
_____
_____

3 What/weather/like/when/you/be/in London?
It/be/cold/and wind/but/it/not rain!
_____
_____

4 If/it/snow/tomorrow/you/cycle to school?
✗ If/it/snow/tomorrow/I/go/by car
_____
_____

.../12

🎧 LISTEN AND CHECK YOUR SCORE

Total	.../40

8 Skills practice

SKILLS FOCUS: READING, LISTENING AND WRITING

Read

1 **Read the texts. What is each person's problem?**

1 _____

2 _____

3 _____

1

Hi Joe,
I'm not enjoying my holiday. The internet connection on the campsite is slow and my mobile phone doesn't work at all. Luckily the weather isn't too bad, but I still don't like camping.
Beth

2

Hi Steve,
What a great hotel. We're near the beach and the internet connection is amazing. That's lucky because it hasn't stopped raining so we haven't been on the beach yet. I don't mind. I can watch films and play games and the food is great!
Jeff

3

Hi Max,
Sorry I haven't emailed before, but this is the first internet café I've found. I brought my new tablet, but there's no internet connection at our apartment. Did you get the text I sent? Why haven't you sent me a reply?
Leanne

2 **Read the texts again and choose the correct options.**

1 There is **no** / **a slow** internet connection on Beth's campsite.

2 Beth doesn't like **the weather** / **camping**.

3 Jeff hasn't been to the beach because **it is too far** / **the weather is bad**.

4 Jeff is **happy** / **upset** with the holiday.

5 Leanne is sending the email from **an internet café** / **her apartment**.

6 Leanne is upset because Max hasn't sent her **an email** / **a text**.

Listen

3 🎧 13 **Listen to the dialogue and number the things that Helen talks about in the correct order.**

a) Travelling ☐

b) The food ☐

c) Computers ☐

d) The weather [1]

e) Mum's problems ☐

f) Free time ☐

4 🎧 13 **Listen again and answer the questions.**

1 Where is Helen?   *In Scotland.*

2 Does she like the food?   _____

3 Has she swum?   _____

4 Has John sent her an email?   _____

5 When are they leaving?   _____

6 What has her mum broken?   _____

Write

5 **Write a letter of thanks. Use the ideas below.**

You were on holiday with your parents and you met someone of your age there. He/She showed you some interesting places, took you to a club and introduced you to his/her friends. Now you are home, write a letter.

- Introduce the letter.
- Describe the journey back home.
- Thank the person for what they did for you and say how much you enjoyed it.
- Say that you hope he/she wants to keep in touch and you definitely will if they write back
- Close the letter.

Dear ….
Hi, it's me, …. I'm the boy/girl who was on holiday in ….

9a Which ones are best?

Vocabulary: Clothes, accessories and styles

1 ⭐ Complete the descriptions with one letter in each space.

Ben is wearing a ¹ *b a s e b a l l* cap, a ² p __ __ __ n, ³ s __ __ __ v __ l __ __ __ top and ⁴ b __ g __ y, ⁵ c __ __ k __ __ trousers.

Lucy has got a ⁶ __ c __ __ f around her neck. She's wearing a ⁷ __ m __ __ t, ⁸ p __ __ t __ __ n __ __ dress and black ⁹ l __ __ g __ __ __ s.

Melissa has got a ¹⁰ c __ __ u __ l top on with a ¹¹ __ __ p in the front and two ¹² p __ __ k __ __ s. She is wearing a ¹³ b __ __ t around the top and ¹⁴ t __ g __ t, ¹⁵ s __ __ t __ __ d trousers.

Phrases

2 ⭐ Complete the dialogues with the words from the box.

> • fortune • more • rubbish • ~~in~~ • case
> • cost • style

1 A: I've got an interview for a summer job.
   B: *In* that _____, wear your new jacket.

2 A: Why didn't you buy those shoes you liked?
   B: They _____ a _____!

3 A: Try this sweater on
   B: No. This one is _____ my _____.

4 A: I don't look good in red.
   B: _____! Red s perfect for you!

Grammar: *Which* + indefinite pronoun *one/ones*

3 ⭐ Complete the dialogues with *one* or *ones*.

1 A: I like these jeans.
   B: Which ¹ *ones*?
   A: The black ² _____.

2 A: There are a lot of nice shirts here.
   B: I know. I don't know which ³ _____ to buy.
   A: These flowery ⁴ _____ are nice.
   B: You're joking!

3 A: I want to wear a hat today.
   B: Which ⁵ _____? Your baseball cap?
   A: No, the ⁶ _____ I bought last summer.

4 A: What are you doing?
   B: I'm throwing away some old clothes. It's difficult to know which ⁷ _____ to throw away and which ⁸ _____ to keep.
   A: Are you going to throw this sweater away?
   B: Which ⁹ _____?
   A: This patterned ¹⁰ _____. I'll have it if you don't want it.

Use your English: Choosing clothes to wear

4 ⭐ **Complete the dialogues with one word in each space.**

1 A: Do you like my new shirt?

   B: Yes, it _looks_ good.

2 A: Do these trousers s_____ me?

   B: No, they're t_____ tight.

3 A: What shall I wear this top w_____?

   B: W_____ don't you try it with these black jeans?

4 A: Which trainers do you p_____?

   B: I think these black ones are best.

5 A: H_____ do I look in this hat?

   B: You l_____ fantastic.

5 ⭐⭐ **Complete the text with the words from the box.**

> • too • don't • reckon • shall • prefer
> • size • look • suit • ones • ~~looks~~

A: I think I'll buy this shirt.

B: Let me see how it [1] _looks_.

A: So, what do you [2] _____? Does it [3] _____ me?

B: No. It's the wrong [4] _____. It's [5] _____ small.

A: But the colour is OK?

B: Yes, that's fine. Try a bigger one.

A: OK.

B: That's better. You [6] _____ great.

A: What [7] _____ I wear with it?

B: Some light trousers.

A: Which [8] _____ do you [9] _____? These or these?

B: I prefer the light grey ones. The brown ones [10] _____ suit you.

A: OK, I'll get the shirt and the trousers. Thanks for your help.

Grammar summary

> **_Which_ + indefinite pronoun _one/ones_**
>
> Do you like this shirt?
> **Which one?**
> The grey **one**.
> Put your shoes on.
> **Which ones?**
> The black **ones**.

Note

Usage

• We use indefinite pronouns to avoid repeating a noun.
  Where's my hat? Which ~~hat~~ one?

• We use _one_ for singular countable nouns and _ones_ for plural nouns.
  That's my house? Which one?
  I'm going to buy some jeans. Which ones?

9b You should go to bed.

Vocabulary: Illness

1 ⭐ **Match the problems to the pictures. Use the correct pronoun.**

> • He/She's got a headache. • He/She's got earache.
> • He/She's got stomachache. • He/She's got toothache.
> • He/She's got a temperature. • He/She's got a sore throat.

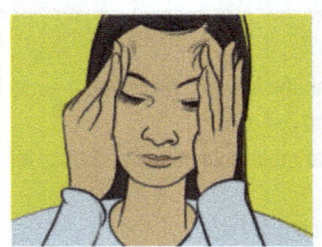

1 *She's got a headache.*

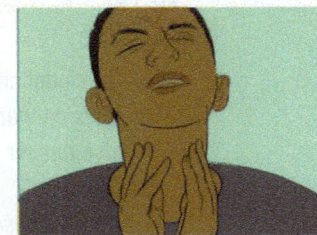

2 _____

3 _____

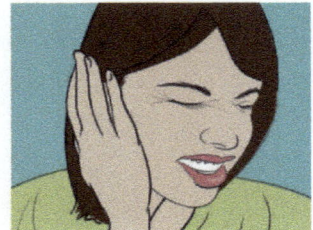

4 _____

5 _____

6 _____

2 ⭐⭐ **Use the prompts and the correct words from the box to write sentences.**

> • … ache • … hurts • … feel …

1 I/tooth   *I've got toothache.*

2 My/ankle   _____

3 I/sick   _____

4 I/not/well   _____

5 I/head   _____

6 My/wrist   _____

7 I/stomach   _____

8 I/ill   _____

9 My/arm   _____

Grammar: Should/Shouldn't

3 ⭐ **Give advice to each person.**

1 **A:** I've got toothache.
   B: (✓ go) *You should go* to the dentist.
   C: (✗ eat) *You shouldn't eat* sweets.

2 **A:** I've got a temperature.
   B: (✓ go) _____ to bed.
   C: (✗ have) _____ a bath.

3 **A:** I've got a sore throat.
   B: (✗ eat) _____ ice cream.
   C: (✓ take) _____ some throat pastilles.

4 **A:** I've got stomachache.
   B: (✗ eat) _____ fast food.
   C: (✓ lie) _____ down.

5 **A:** I feel sick.
   B: (✓ go) _____ to the bathroom.
   C: (✗ go) _____ to school.

6 **A:** I've got a headache.
   B: (✗ use) _____ your computer.
   C: (✓ take) _____ a painkiller.

7 **A:** I've got a cough.
   B: (✓ take) _____ some cough mixture.
   C: (✗ play) _____ football.

8 **A:** I've got earache.
   B: (✓ phone) _____ the doctor.
   C: (✗ put) _____ your finger in your ear!

4 ⭐⭐ **Use the prompts to complete the dialogues.**

A: My friend is having a lot of problems at school.
   ¹ (What/I/do?) *What should I do?*

B: ² (You/talk) _____ to
   her. ³ (She/tell) _____
   her parents and her teacher. ⁴ (She/not/say)
   _____ things are OK and
   hope that the problem will go away. It won't.

A: My friends are going to a concert on Friday.
   My parents told me that I can't go. ⁵ (I/tell)
   _____ them I'm going to
   the cinema, but go to the concert?

B: ⁶ (✗) _____. ⁷ (You/not/lie)
   _____ to your parents. It's
   wrong.

A: I've got exams soon, but I like going
   out and meeting my friends. ⁸ (I/stop)
   _____ going out and stay at
   home studying?

B: ⁹ (✓) _____.
   Exams are important. ¹⁰ (You/work)
   _____ hard and meet your
   friends after the exams.

Grammar summary

Should/Shouldn't

Affirmative	Negative
You **should work** harder. We **should leave** soon.	He **shouldn't go** to school today. They **shouldn't swim** in this weather.
Questions	**Short answers**
Should I **go** to bed?	Yes, you **should**. No, you **shouldn't**.

Wh- questions
What **should** I **wear**? Who **should** I **talk** to?

Note

Usage
- We use *should/shouldn't* to give advice.
  You should do more exercise.
  You shouldn't wear that shirt.

Form
- In affirmative sentences, we use *should* + infinitive without *to*.
  We should go by bus.
- In negative sentences, we use *shouldn't* + infinitive without *to*.
  We shouldn't stay out late.
- To make questions, we reverse the order of *should* and the subject.
  I should leave. Should I leave?
- In short answers, we do not repeat the main verb.
  Should I ask my mum?
  Yes, you should. NOT *Yes, you should ask.*

Common mistakes
~~What I should do?~~ ✗
What should I do? ✓
~~You shouldn't to be late.~~ ✗
You shouldn't be late. ✓

9c We have to make our beds.

Vocabulary: Household jobs

1 ⭐ **Look at the picture and complete the sentences.**

1 Harold is doing the *vacuuming*.

2 Marjorie is doing the _____.

3 Tom is doing the _____.

4 Emily is doing the _____.

5 Sally is doing the _____.

2 ⭐⭐ **Match the beginnings (1–7) to the endings (a–g).**

1 do	a) the dishwasher.
2 make	b) your room.
3 tidy	c) the car.
4 lay	d) the rubbish out.
5 empty	e) the shopping.
6 take	f) the table.
7 wash	g) your bed.

Grammar: Have to/Don't have to

3 ⭐ **Look at the information and complete the text.**

> **Jobs list:**
>
> | | Jack | Ellen |
> |---|---|---|
> | Tidy room | ✓ | ✓ |
> | Lay table | ✓ | ✗ |
> | Empty dishwasher | ✗ | ✓ |
> | Make breakfast | ✗ | ✓ |
> | Wash car | ✓ | ✗ |
> | Make bed | ✓ | ✓ |

Jack and Ellen [1] *have* to tidy their rooms every Saturday. Jack [2] _____ the table every day. Ellen [3] _____ the table, but she [4] _____ the dishwasher. Jack [5] _____ the dishwasher and he [6] _____ breakfast. Ellen [7] _____ breakfast. Jack [8] _____ the car on Sundays. Jack and Ellen [9] _____ their beds every day before they go to school.

4 ⭐⭐ **Complete the dialogue with the correct form of *have to* or *don't have to*.**

A: Hi Jack. What household jobs [1] (you/do) *do you have to do*?

B: [2] (I/tidy/room) _____ every week and [3] (I/make/bed) _____ every day.

A: [4] (you/make/breakfast) _____?

B: [5] (✗) _____. [6] (My sister/do) _____ that, but [7] (I/lay) _____ the table.

A: [8] (you/do/washing-up) _____?

B: [9] (✗) _____. We've got a dishwasher. [10] (I/not/empty) _____ that because my sister does it. What about you? [11] (you/do) _____ a lot of jobs in the house?

A: [12] (✓) _____.

104

Grammar: *Want to, want* + object pronoun + *to*

5 ⭐⭐ **Rewrite the sentences with *want*.**

> Debbie, can you help me choose a dress for the prom? Thanks. Ellie

1 Ellie *wants Debbie to help* her choose a dress for the prom.

> Simon, how about going swimming this Saturday? Nathan

2 Nathan _____

with him on Saturday.

> Ed. Please get some milk on your way home. Mum and Dad

3 Ed's parents _____

some milk on his way home.

> Jack + Will. Meet us outside the cinema at 7 p.m. Emma + Cathy xxx

4 Emma and Cathy _____

_____ them outside the cinema at 7 p.m.

> Class 6C. Please work quietly while I talk to a parent.

5 Class 6C's teacher _____

_____ while she talks to a parent.

> Mum, I'll do the washing-up, but can I not lay the table? Jenny

6 Jenny _____ the

washing-up, but she _____

the table.

Grammar summary

Have to/Don't have to	
Affirmative	**Negative**
I **have to** get up at 6 a.m. He **has to** cook dinner.	You **don't have to** go home. She **doesn't have to** leave.
Questions	**Short answers**
Do you **have to** do the ironing? **Does** he **have to** go to bed early?	Yes, I **do**. No, I **don't**. Yes, he **does**. No, he **doesn't**.

> **Note**
>
> **Usage**
> - We use *have/has to* to say something is necessary.
>   *I have to make my bed.*
> - We use *don't/doesn't have to* to say that something is not necessary.
>   *I don't have to get up early.*
>
> **Form**
> - In affirmative sentences, we use *have/has to* + infinitive without *to*.
>   *She has to do the shopping.*
> - In negative sentences, we use *don't/doesn't* + *have to* + infinitive without *to*
>   *We don't have to leave yet.*
> - In questions, we use *Do/Does* + subject + *have to* + infinitive without *to*.
>   *Do you have to make your bed?*

Want to, want + object pronoun + to

I **want to go** to sleep.
She **wants me to help** her.

> **Note**
>
> **Form**
> - We use *want* (+ object pronoun) + *to* + infinitive
>   *I want to listen to this CD.*
>   *I want them to listen.*

9 Language round-up

1 Complete the sentences with one word in each space.

> ### To do list
> 1 _Make_ my bed.
> 2 T_____ the rubbish out.
> 3 L_____ the table.
> 4 E _____ the dishwasher.
> 5 W_____ the car.
> 6 D_____ the shopping.
>
> ### Shopping list
> Chemist's
> Something for Mum's 7 s_____ throat
> Some 8 c_____ mixture
> Something for James, who 9 f _____ sick
>
> ### Clothes shopping
> A new baseball 10 c _____
> A cool T-shirt - 11 o _____ that doesn't cost a 12 f _____!

.../11

2 Complete the text with the words from the box.

> • ones (x2) • don't • prefer • to
> • have • looked • too • size • style
> • suit

I bought some new trainers today. The 1 _ones_ which I bought last year are 2 _____ small for me now. I'm a 3 _____ 44! I tried some black trainers but they didn't 4 _____ me. I 5 _____ white 6 _____. They are more my 7 _____. In the end I found some. They 8 _____ great and I really wanted 9 _____ buy them. I 10 _____ have to pay all the money now. I paid £10 and I 11 _____ to pay £5 a month for a year.

.../10

3 Write short answers.

1 Should I phone the doctor?
✓ _Yes, you should._

2 Do you have to go to bed early?
✗ _____

3 Does your mum want me to leave?
✗ _____

4 Should I take some cough mixture?
✗ _____

5 Does she look good in this hat?
✓ _____

6 Do your parents have to work at the weekend?
✗ _____

.../10

4 Put the words in the correct order to make questions.

1 you/do/do/ironing/have/the/to
Do you have to do the ironing?

2 which/prefer/one/you/do
_____

3 suit/this/does/me/shirt
_____

4 skirt/shall/this/what/with/wear/I
_____

5 dress/do/this/I/how/in/look
_____

6 wear/I/to/should/party/what/the
_____

7 should/much/I/how/mixture/cough/take
_____

8 the/sister/dishwasher/does/have/your/to/empty
_____

9 to/what/have/jobs/you/do/household/do
_____

10 do/do/to/what/you/me/want
_____

.../9

🎧 14 LISTEN AND CHECK YOUR SCORE	
Total	.../40

9 Skills practice

SKILLS FOCUS: READING AND WRITING

Read

1 Read the text. Which teenager has a problem with some other people?

a) Sammy   b) Colin   c) Miranda

I've got an interview for a summer job. I've never had an interview before. Should I dress very smartly or can I be casual, but clean? I'm going to work in the kitchen of a restaurant, doing the washing-up and cleaning. Please help. I really want this job. **Sammy**

I'm happy at school, but some people in my class laugh at my clothes. I know my clothes aren't 'cool', but I think they suit me. What should I do or say to the other students or should I just not listen to them? **Colin**

I'm a student in Year 12 of school. I don't often have time to go out because we have a lot of homework to do. I also learn the guitar and Spanish after school. I've started getting headaches. Should I go to the doctor or should I just try to do a bit less? **Miranda**

2 Read the text again and answer true (T), false (F) or doesn't say (DS).

1 Sammy works in a restaurant at the moment. *F*

2 Sammy isn't going to be a waiter. ___

3 Colin hasn't got any friends in his class. ___

4 Colin doesn't like the clothes he wears. ___

5 Miranda often meets her friends. ___

6 Miranda hasn't been to see the doctor yet. ___

Write

3 Complete the letter with the words from the box.

- don't • think • few • everyone
- ~~opinion~~ • most

Dear Sir/Madam,

I read your article about health last week. In my [1] *opinion*, some of the things you wrote were wrong. I [2] _____ the problem is that people don't take care of their health. [3] _____ knows that young people eat more fast food and do less exercise than young people ten or twenty years ago. [4] _____ of my friends eat fast food once a week and a [5] _____ have fast food every day for lunch. I [6] _____ think we need better medicine or more doctors. We need healthier lives.

Yours,

Jemima Sparks

4 Match the beginnings (1–6) to the endings (a–e). Two beginnings match the same ending.

1 In my   a) think that …
2 I   b) knows that …
3 Everybody   c) opinion …
4 I don't   d) of my friends …
5 A   e) few people …
6 Some

5 You have read an article that says there shouldn't be school uniforms. You don't agree. Write a letter giving your opinions and reasons for them.

Dear Sir/Madam,

I am writing about your article on school uniforms.

Notes

Notes

Notes

Notes

Notes